Bible

Stories

with

End Time

Parallels

Larry W. Wilson

**Wake Up America Seminars, Inc.
P.O. Box 273, Bellbrook, Ohio 45305
(937) 848-3322**

Cover: Comstock.com

October 2002
Second Printing, November 2009

Bible Stories
with End Time Parallels

Table of Contents

Forward

Nothing excites me more than to discover deeper insight from the Scriptures. As I began to focus my study on prophecy, I was amazed how many well-known Bible stories have such profound end time parallels. The ten stories in this book were originally published in the monthly newsletter *Day Star* during the first ten months of 2002. I have compiled the stories in this book for three reasons: First, I hope this book will be widely distributed, because I want everyone to know that the Bible has never been more relevant and timely than it is right now! I know many other Bible stories have end time parallels, but I have chosen these particular stories because they are so rich in content. As these stories are placed in proper context, it is much easier to understand *how* and *why* God's people will be tested during the Great Tribulation. Second, I want you to know enough background information about the character in each story to feel as though you were there when the story took place. Understanding the tests, struggles, mistakes and victories of the Bible characters presented in each story should encourage and prepare us for the days ahead. Last, I want you to know that faith in God means to submit to His demands and remain loyal to Him in the face of life-threatening adversity. If any concept stands out in this book, I hope it is this point: Faith in God is much more than believing there is a God. (The demons know there is a God and they tremble because of it! James 2:19)

When people truly love God, their everyday actions will reflect a dedicated commitment to uphold and honor the ways of God, which are quite different from the focus and goals that this world honors. (A child of God is known by his actions. 1 John 3:10) A faith-filled Christian often stands in direct opposition to what the world holds in high esteem (Romans 8:7); therefore, honoring God is not always a pleasant experience. The pressures to conform to the world's status quo explains, in part, why ancient Israel frequently apostatized. (2 Kings 17:15) Even more, the priests of Israel failed to lead the nation to understand that as a people and a nation, they must be vigilant because humankind is inherently rebellious toward God. (Ezekiel 22:26) When the forces of our carnal nature and the pressures to conform to the ways of the world are combined, serving God becomes a big challenge and requires *patient* faith. (James 1:3) God understands our dilemma. This is why He preserved so many stories of faith in the Bible. Unless we examine and understand the failures and the victories of our forefathers, we will repeat their mistakes.

The Bible is clear – salvation comes through faith in God. (Ephesians 2:8,9) Given this sublime truth, I hope you will gain a new appreciation about many aspects of faith as you read this book. Faith in God is so much more than intellectual assent or agreement with fact. Faith in God leads to adventure and fills your heart with peace and joy. True happiness springs from knowing and loving the great "I AM" – the One who first loved us.

Larry Wilson

October, 2002

Chapter 1

Daniel – A Test of Loyalty

Someone once said that loyalty is like the juice of an orange –
the flavor cannot be determined until the orange is squeezed to
the breaking point. The Bible testifies to the truthfulness of this
statement. Loyalty is one of the powerful forces within the
human heart. Circumstances can *squeeze* us to a point that we
reveal our highest loyalties. Loyalty can produce good results as
well as evil results. Many examples in the Bible demonstrate
both results: Judas Iscariot was loyal to his dreams of self-
importance, power and wealth, instead of humility, poverty and
service. When he realized that following Jesus would not fulfill
his dreams, he betrayed the Savior of the world for $12.60 (30
pieces of silver). For awhile, King David was loyal to his passions for Bathsheba. He killed her husband, Uriah, who was one
of his most loyal soldiers, so he could hide his illicit affair with
Bathsheba and cover her subsequent pregnancy with the cloak
of marriage. Peter swore his loyalty to Jesus was 100%, but
when he learned that he might have to share a martyr's death
with Jesus, he denied three times that he even knew Jesus. The
Philippian jailer was loyal to his job until an earthquake destroyed his jail, which suddenly changed his heart. Saul was
loyal to his religion – faithfully persecuting apostate Jews (a.k.a.
Christians) – until Jesus confronted him on the road to Damascus. Afterwards, Paul proved to have unwavering loyalty to
Jesus. He suffered extreme persecution from both the Jews and
Romans, as he preached salvation through Jesus Christ. Eventu-
ally, Nero sentenced him to death because of his loyalty to Jesus.
Shadrach, Meshach and Abednego chose to be loyal to the God of
Heaven rather than worship the golden image, and for their
decision, Nebuchadnezzar threw them into the fiery furnace.
John the Baptist was loyal to God's standards when he plainly

told King Herod that living with his brother's wife was a sin, and his remarks cost him his life. King Saul almost killed his own son, Jonathan, because of Jonathan's loyalty to David's Heavenly anointing. Jeremiah was loyal to the Word of the Lord when he told the people the truth about their apostasy, and his own people threw him into a cistern to die. Job's loyalty to God was tested with some of the harshest suffering ever recorded. Noah was loyal to God's command and suffered an incredible amount of ridicule, but his loyalty and faith saved his family. Ruth was loyal to Naomi by choosing to suffer with her in poverty, but this action made her an ancestor of Jesus. Rahab, the prostitute, was loyal to the spies who entered Jericho, but by doing so, she saved her family. Queen Esther was loyal to her people and ultimately became instrumental in delivering them from destruction. The prophet Daniel was another man of loyalty who was *squeezed* hard. He chose to defy the decree of his king by openly praying toward Jerusalem and for this small act, he was thrown into the lion's den.

Webster's definition of loyalty states that loyalty means being constant and faithful, bearing true allegiance to something. The truth is, every human being has loyalties, but the real question is, "To what or whom are we loyal?" *Our highest loyalties are revealed when we are squeezed into a decision that favors one loyalty and harms another.* Thoughtfully review the first paragraph and notice how certain people had to make some very difficult choices. Inevitably, we all face situations where circumstances leave no option but to favor a higher loyalty and harm a lesser one! For this reason, it is hard to say where our highest loyalties really lie until we are "squeezed" by difficult choices. (The process of "squeezing" explains why there will be a Great Tribulation. God is going to "squeeze" the loyalty out of every human being to see who loves Him above everything else. See Revelation 3:10.)

I thought a Bible study on Daniel and his lion's den experience might prove helpful as we focus on the subject of loyalty. Most Christians have rejoiced in the story of Daniel's escape from the lions, but few people know the bigger picture. Daniel's loyalty had a profound impact on two significant nations! To make this story as compelling as possible, I have added background information to help you "stand in Daniel's sandals."

A Prisoner of War

Daniel was taken to Babylon as a prisoner of war as a result of Nebuchadnezzar's first siege on Jerusalem in 605 B.C. It is believed that Daniel was about 17 or 18 years of age. It was King Nebuchadnezzar's policy to take the best captives and enroll them in an academy to prepare them for government service. The king had wisely established a school to train captives from various tribal nations, so the captives could eventually return to their homeland and serve the empire of Babylon as rulers who were loyal to the king of Babylon. It was for this purpose that Daniel and some of his friends were inducted into the king's academy. The book of Daniel begins with Daniel and his closest friends asking the king's steward if they could be excused from eating at the king's table. They wanted to maintain a more simple, vegetarian diet, but the steward refused this first request. He was sure that Daniel and his friends would become sick and feeble if they ate nothing but vegetables and water. If they became sick because of his negligence, he could lose his job or possibly, his head! However, Daniel persisted and eventually, the steward gave in. When the time came for the king to test the trainees, Daniel and his friends were found to be at the top of their class. In fact, the Bible conservatively estimates their knowledge was ten times better than their fellow students. (Daniel 1) Do you think the success of Daniel and his friends had anything to do with their loyalty to God? I do.

A short time later, Daniel gained worldwide recognition when God used him to interpret a dream that God gave to Nebuchadnezzar. As a result of that incident, Nebuchadnezzar promoted Daniel to a very high government position and all the *wise* men of Babylon reported to him. (Daniel 2) Do you think that Daniel's success had anything to do with his loyalty to God? I do.

Why Was Daniel Sent to Babylon?

Historians tell us that Nebuchadnezzar set siege to Jerusalem three times. He finally destroyed the city in 586 B.C. because Israel's kings refused to submit to Nebuchadnezzar's "higher" authority. In actuality, God allowed Jerusalem to be destroyed and its citizens put in captivity for 70 years because Israel refused to submit to God's "higher" authority. The Bible carefully justifies God's anger with Israel. To understand God's wrath against Israel in 605 B.C., we must start with Moses. Carefully read these texts:

1. Sabbath Rest Required for the Land - Leviticus 25

A few weeks after the Exodus, **"The Lord said to Moses on Mount Sinai, 'Speak to the Israelites and say to them: 'When you enter the land I am going to give you, the land itself must observe a Sabbath to the Lord. For six years sow your fields, and for six years prune your vineyards and gather their crops. But in the seventh year the land is to have a Sabbath of rest, a Sabbath to the Lord. Do not sow your fields or prune your vineyards. Do not reap what grows of itself or harvest the grapes of your untended vines. The land is to have a year of rest.' "** (Leviticus 25:1-5) This text is self explanatory. God required the land to rest every seventh year. Why would any nation refuse a year's vacation every seventh year? The Lord continues, **"You may ask, 'What will we eat in the seventh year if we do not plant or harvest our crops?' I will send you such a blessing in the sixth year that the land will yield enough for three years. While you plant during the eighth year, you will eat from the old crop and will continue to eat from it until the harvest of the ninth year comes in."** (Leviticus 25:20-22) There is a profound point in these verses: God promised to send a bumper crop every sixth year so there would be enough food to observe a year of rest! Contrary to what many Bible students say, the Sabbath rest for the land was not for agricultural purposes. In fact, God made the land produce its greatest harvest during the sixth year – when the land was in its most exhausted condition! The lesson to be learned from the Sabbath year is simple. God established the Sabbath year rest *to test* His people. There is no other reason. Would they be loyal or rebellious? (See Exodus 16 for a parallel concerning the seventh day.)

2. If You Don't Keep My Sabbath Years - Leviticus 26

God also warned Israel: **"If in spite of this** [lesser punishments] **you still do not listen to me but continue to be hostile toward me, then in my anger I will be hostile toward you, and I myself will punish you for your sins seven times over. . . . I will turn your cities into ruins and lay waste your sanctuaries, and I will take no delight in the pleasing aroma of your offerings. I will lay waste the land, so that your enemies who live there will be appalled. I will scatter you among the nations and will draw out my sword and pursue you. Your land will be laid waste, and your cities will lie in ruins. Then the land will enjoy its sabbath years all the time that it lies desolate and you are in the country of your enemies; then the land will rest and enjoy its sabbaths. All the time that it lies desolate, the land will have the rest it did not have during the sabbaths you lived in it."** (Leviticus 26:27,28,31-35, insertion mine) It does not take a rocket scientist to understand these words. God said the land was going to rest, with or without Israel. God wanted His people to understand a profound truth: **". . .** [The Lord said] **the land is mine and you are but aliens and my tenants."** (Leviticus 25:23, insertion mine) God wanted Israel to know that their occupation of His land was conditional on their steadfast loyalty to Him. (Leviticus 18; Deuteronomy 28)

3. Because You Have Rebelled - Jeremiah 25

The Old Testament indicates over and over again that Israel did not remain loyal to God. Their cup of disobedience overflowed and around 615 B.C. God gave a prophecy to Jeremiah: He said, **" 'I will summon all the peoples of the north and my servant Nebuchadnezzar king of Babylon,' declares the**

Lord, 'and I will bring them against this land and its inhabitants and against all the surrounding nations. I will completely destroy them and make them an object of horror and scorn, and an everlasting ruin. I will banish from them the sounds of joy and gladness, the voices of bride and bridegroom, the sound of millstones and the light of the lamp. This whole country will become a desolate wasteland, and these nations will serve the king of Babylon seventy years. But when the seventy years are fulfilled, I will punish the king of Babylon and his nation, the land of the Babylonians, for their guilt,' declares the Lord, 'and will make it desolate forever.' " (Jeremiah 25:9-12) Notice three things: First, God calls King Nebuchadnezzar "My servant." This is an important concept. God chose a pagan king to be an agent of His wrath against Jerusalem. (Parallel: The Antichrist will be an agent of God's wrath druing the Great Tribulation.) Second, God said that Jerusalem would be destroyed and that Israel would be prisoners of war in Babylon for 70 years. Third, Babylon – for the same sins as Jerusalem – would eventually be destroyed.

4. 430 Years of Rebellion

During the 70 years of captivity in Babylon, God anointed two prophets, Daniel and Ezekiel. Ezekiel was a prisoner of war like Daniel, but Ezekiel lived among the captives, while Daniel lived in the halls of power. Ezekiel was timid and afraid of public speaking, so the Lord prompted him to "act out" various signs for Israel to watch. Notice this sign: ". . . **This will be a sign to the house of Israel. . .** [Ezekiel] **lie on your left side and put the sin of the house of Israel upon yourself. You are to bear their sin for the number of days you lie on your side. I have assigned you the same number of days as the years of their sin. So for 390 days you will bear the sin of the house of Israel. After you have finished this, lie down again, this time on your right side, and bear the sin of the house of Judah. I have assigned you 40 days, a day for each year.**" (Ezekiel 4:3,6, insertion mine) This text is important because God indicates the length of rebellion of the twelve tribes as 430 years. (390 + 40 = 430)   This number should catch your attention because it is the same number of years that Israel spent in Egypt. (Exodus 12:41) These two separate and distinct instances of 430 years have three things in common: apostasy, timing and vigil. First, the apostasy of the Israelites in Egypt is no different than the apostasy of the Israelites in the promised land of Canaan! Apostasy is always the course of fallen man. Second, God's timing is perfect in both instances. The Bible says that God delivered the Israelites from Egyptian slavery according to His promise to Abraham, exactly 430 years *to the very day*. (Exodus 12:41) If God delivered Israel from Egypt on time, then it should be no surprise that He sent them into captivity on time as well. It should be noted that when Israel violated 70 Sabbath years, God sent them into captivity! How do we know this? Ezekiel performed the "430 day" sign for all of Israel to see. There are exactly 70 Sabbatical years in 430 years. In other words, the Babylonian captivity was 70 years in length because that is the exact number of Sabbath years Israel violated. Remember God's threat in Leviticus 26:34,35? **"Then the land will enjoy its Sabbath years all the time that it lies desolate and you are in the country of your enemies; then the land will rest and enjoy its Sabbaths. All the time that it lies desolate, the land will have the rest it did not have during the Sabbaths you lived in it."** This text demonstrates the last significant point in common between these separate 430 year periods. God keeps vigil. He does not sleep. He is very much aware of everything that takes place on Earth and He will step into the affairs of men when the timing is just right. He delivered Israel from slavery in Egypt during the right year, and He sent Israel into Babylonnian captivity on time and during the right year! Furthermore, the next text demonstrates that God also delivered Israel out of their Babylonian captivity during the right year and right on time.

5. Prophecy Fulfilled

The Bible says, **"God handed all of them** [the Jews] **over to Nebuchadnezzar. He carried to Babylon all the articles** from the temple of God, both large and small, and the treasures of the Lord's temple and the treasures of the king and his officials. They set fire to God's temple and broke down the wall of Jerusalem; they burned all the palaces and destroyed everything of value there. He carried into exile to Babylon the remnant, who escaped from the sword, and they became servants to him and his sons until the kingdom of Persia came to power. The land enjoyed its sabbath rests; all the time of its desolation it rested, until the seventy years were completed in fulfillment of the word of the Lord spoken by Jeremiah." (2 Chronicles 36:17-21, insertion mine) Again, the reason for the Babylonian captivity is simple and obvious. God handed Israel over to Nebuchadnezzar because of their disloyalty. They refused to keep His Sabbaths, so He evicted them and the land rested for 70 years.

Zooming Forward

Now that we understand *why* Israel went into Babylonian captivity, we need to zoom forward in time to the fall of Babylon, when Nebuchadnezzar's reign ended. Historians say Babylon fell on Tishri 16 (around October 13), 539 B.C. Darius came to the throne during that year (his ascension year), so his first calendar year (according to the religious calendar of the Jews) was 538/7 B.C. The first year of Darius' reign is Daniel's 68th year in captivity. Daniel was taken captive during 605 B.C., a "Sabbath year," and he calculated that the 70 years of desolation decreed upon Jerusalem would end on the "Friday year," 536 B.C. (Counting inclusively, 605 B.C. minus 536 B.C. equals 70 years.)

Note: When God established the week of years at the time of the Exodus, God required Israel to set their slaves free every sixth or "Friday year." The seventh or "Sabbath year" was to be celebrated as a year of freedom from the bondage of slavery. (See Exodus 21:2 and Jeremiah 34:14-16.) Daniel was aware of the Jubilee calendar. He also understood how the "week of years" synchronized and knew that 536/5 B.C. was a "Friday year," as well as the 70th or final year of captivity.

The Political Situation in Daniel's 68th Year

It was extremely unusual in ancient times for a conquering king to give a prisoner of war a position of authority in his government. The possibility of rebellion was just too great. Incredible as it seems, this happened to Daniel three times that we know of. Nebuchadnezzar promoted Daniel to one of his highest governing positions after Daniel interpreted his dream. Belteshazzar promoted Daniel to one of his highest governing positions after Daniel read the handwriting on the wall. Daniel was also promoted to one of the highest positions in the kingdom when Darius became king. Do you think Daniel's promotions had anything to do with his loyalty to God? I do.

It is my understanding that Daniel believed God had placed him in a very powerful political position within the government of Darius so that *he, Daniel,* might facilitate Israel's release from captivity. However, Daniel was nearing 90 years of age and knew that if he acted on his own wisdom, he could interfere with God's plans, just as Moses did when he wrongfully killed the Egyptian. (Exodus 2:11-14) Daniel also knew that if his actions backfired, it could result in a lot of suffering for his people, just as it did when Moses and Aaron ordered the Hebrew slaves to rest from their labors. (Exodus 5:5) Daniel was acutely aware that he could dishonor God if his actions to free his people aroused suspicion, jealousy or any hint of rebellion against the Medes and Persians. Many of the Chaldeans intensely hated the Jews, and any move on Daniel's part to free his people would probably be construed as treason. If this occurred and he was convicted in a court of public opinion, the punishment was sudden death.

> **Note:** About 70 years after Daniel died, the Chaldeans' hatred for the Jews escalated on a national scale. The noble, Haman, obtained a universal death decree from King Artaxerxes for all Jews in the Persian kingdom, but God used Queen Esther to save her people.

Daniel's dilemma had other ramifications. During the 70 years of captivity in Babylon, the Jews multiplied and integrated into the fabric of the province of Babylon. Some Jews prospered and others remained servants or slaves of the Chaldeans. When Darius began his reign over Babylon, most of the original captives from Jerusalem had died. Therefore, their offspring who lived in Babylon had little attachment to a place where they had never lived or even seen. In fact, when Cyrus set the Jews free in 536 B.C., Ezra 2 indicates that only a minority of captives, 29,818 Jewish males, returned to Jerusalem.

The Greatest Problems

Politically, Daniel knew that the emancipation of his people after 70 years in Babylon could cause a number of problems for King Darius. If many Chaldeans lost their servants, they would incur financial losses, which would produce terrible social unrest. Daniel was also aware that during the 70 years of desolation, tribal nations had moved into the territory abandoned by Israel, and a *returning* Israel could be embroiled in wars and land disputes. Even more, the greatest cause of concern for Daniel was that Darius did not rule over the land of Canaan where Jerusalem was located. Any decree that freed the Jews from the province of Babylon would also require a decree by King Cyrus, who ruled over Canaan. The ultimate goal, of course, was that the Jews recover the land they had lost, and all the circumstances surrounding this situation greatly perplexed Daniel. What could *he* do to facilitate the freedom of his people? Even if they were set free, how could Daniel motivate a majority of the Jews to return to Jerusalem? Daniel's mind churned over these issues for months because he could see how a significant exodus from Babylon could be a political nightmare for King Darius, as well as King Cyrus.

Jealousy Knows No Bounds

From Daniel's point of view, the upcoming 70th year, 536/5 B.C., would not be a very good year to attempt the release of the Jews. Even though Daniel held one of the highest positions in the empire, a new king was on the throne. This meant a new administration was in place adhering to a new set of laws and corporate culture, which included a large group of powerful nobles who hated the Jews. As Daniel pondered his helpless position, it became apparent to him that Israel's deliverance from slavery would have to be an "Act of God," a miracle as great as the exodus from Egypt. To his credit, Daniel faithfully carried out his responsibilities within Darius' administration. The Bible says of this time-period, **"Now Daniel so distinguished himself among the administrators and the satraps by his exceptional qualities that the king planned to set him over the whole kingdom."** (Daniel 6:3)

Sometime during Darius' first calendar year (538/7 B.C.), Daniel decided the best thing he could do was seek God through fasting, praying and wearing sackcloth and ashes. Time was running out! The 70th year was approaching fast. So, Daniel sought the Lord in utter humility to see what God wanted of him. To be seen in sackcloth and ashes was a sign of mourning or extreme humiliation. To the Medes and Persians, Daniel's appearance must have been very odd since Daniel usually wore clothing appropriate for his exalted office. Regardless, Daniel embarrassed (humbled) himself before God as a man in sackcloth and ashes demonstrating that God could use him in whatever meaningful or menial way God desired.

Unknown to Daniel, King Darius had planned to promote Daniel above the other two governors of his empire. Darius decided to do this because he had contracted a degenerating health problem. Darius favored Daniel because Daniel was "pure in heart," a very unusual quality among people in politics, then and now. Darius also wanted to make Daniel, "the Jew," his number two man in the kingdom because this would strategically protect his throne when he became too weak to meet the day to day needs of his office. Unlike the other two administrators, Darius knew Daniel would be loyal to him instead of having an inner ambition to acquire the throne. Besides, Darius knew that a Jew would not aspire to be king over an empire of Medes and Persians. By putting Daniel in the number two seat, his throne would be safer from the schemes of ambitious politicians and administrators.

Somehow, this information about Darius' plans was leaked to the administrators and they were filled with jealousy and rage. No self respecting Mede or Persian would be subject to a Jew! Jealousy and hatred for Daniel, "the Jew," led them to search for anything they could use to marr Daniel's reputation and disqualify him from such a position of honor. They studied Daniel's personal history and tried to find a flaw in his character, but were unable to find anything. The Bible says, **"At this, the administrators and the satraps tried to find grounds for charges against Daniel in his conduct of government affairs, but they were unable to do so. They could find no corruption in him, because he was trustworthy and neither corrupt nor negligent. Finally these men said, 'We will never find any basis for charges against this man Daniel unless it has something to do with the law of his God.' "** (Daniel 6:4,5) Given the hatred and determination of his enemies and the notorious behavior of politicians down through the ages, these are amazing words!

Putting the Squeeze on Daniel

Finally, the administrators and satraps concluded that the only way to stop Darius from promoting Daniel was to *prove* to Darius that Daniel's loyalty to his "Jewish" God was higher than Daniel's loyalty to the king. They figured the question of loyalty would prove their point to Darius. When it comes to politics, kings have to be gods. Their ego and government rests upon nothing less than total submission and devotion to their will. If no one wants to obey the king, how can he be king? Therefore, "loyalty tests" were used by ancient kings to ferret out people with bad attitudes toward the authority of the king. This may explain why Darius did not quibble or hesitate to issue a loyalty decree. Loyalty tests were simple: During the specified month, suspects were arraigned and questioned before a court of political leaders. If the suspect freely confessed allegiance to the king as the highest authority on Earth, the suspect would then affirm his loyalty to the king with an oath. However, if the suspect was hostile toward the king or plotting rebellion, a "loyalty test" became a life and death issue, even though the suspect may not

have been caught doing anything wrong. This is why loyalty
tests were so effective. If the suspect refused to take an oath
affirming his allegiance and submission to the king, he was
declared a rebel and killed immediately. On the other hand, if
he lied about his allegiance to the king and gave an oath of
loyalty, his sympathizers would see that he was a common
coward and a liar. Who could respect such a disgusting person?
This technique for testing loyalty was simple and effective.
Incidently, the Caesars also used loyalty tests. Thousands of
Christians perished because they would not bow down before the
"man-god," Caesar. (John 19:15; Romans 10:9) During the
Great Tribulation, God will also use a simple loyalty test. A test
of worship will put the "squeeze" on every person and our deep-
est loyalties will be "squeezed out" for everyone to see. (See
Revelation 13:8-18.)

The Perfect Plot

The crafty administrators asked Darius for permission to conduct a "loyalty check" for three reasons: First, a loyalty test was
a well-known tactic. Since the province of Babylon was a new
territory for Darius, a loyalty test appeared to be a "good idea" to
help secure his throne. Second, if Daniel should slip through the
30 day decree trap, Darius would never know the real motives
behind the administrators request for the loyalty test. Third, if
Daniel was caught in their trap, he would be "legally" killed
because the law demanded the sudden death of anyone caught in
rebellion against the king. If Daniel was destroyed, the administrators would not be implicated in Daniel's death. The "loyalty test"
seemed like the perfect way to eliminate Daniel, or so they thought.

When the administrators asked the king for a loyalty decree,
they must have known that Darius did not know about Daniel's
current state of humiliation. If Darius had been aware of
Daniel's behavior, praying to his God three times a day in sackcloth and ashes, this knowledge would have foiled their plot. **"So
the administrators and the satraps went as a group to
the king and said: 'O King Darius, live forever! The royal
administrators, prefects, satraps, advisers and governors**

have all agreed that the king should issue an edict and enforce the decree that anyone who prays to any god or man during the next thirty days, except to you, O king, shall be thrown into the lions' den. Now, O king, issue the decree and put it in writing so that it cannot be altered–in accordance with the laws of the Medes and Persians, which cannot be repealed.' So King Darius put the decree in writing." (Daniel 9:6-9)

Daniel Springs the Trap

"Now when Daniel learned that the decree had been published, he went home to his upstairs room where the windows opened toward Jerusalem. Three times a day he got down on his knees and prayed, giving thanks to his God, just as he had done before. Then these men went as a group and found Daniel praying and asking God for help. So they went to the king and spoke to him about his royal decree: 'Did you not publish a decree that during the next thirty days anyone who prays to any god or man except to you, O king, would be thrown into the lions' den?' The king answered, 'The decree stands–in accordance with the laws of the Medes and Persians, which cannot be repealed.' Then they said to the king, 'Daniel, who is one of the exiles from Judah, pays no attention to you, O king, or to the decree you put in writing. He still prays three times a day.' When the king heard this, he was greatly distressed; he was determined to rescue Daniel and made every effort until sundown to save him." (Daniel 6:10-14)

Did you notice how fast Daniel *willfully* disobeyed the king's decree? Why did one of the kingdom's highest officials publically defy the law of the king? The answer lies in the fact that Daniel understood the reasons behind the *loyalty test*. Daniel remembered his three friends and their fiery furnace test, and he knew he was being tested just like his three friends. Evidently, Daniel was notified of the decree suddenly and without warning. I find it interesting that Daniel did not go to his immediate superior,

King Darius and plead his case! When Daniel learned of the loyalty test, he ran to (not from) his prayer room. This action says volumes about Daniel's loyalty to the God of Heaven!

When Daniel humbled himself before God and man by wearing sackcloth and ashes, Daniel's heart was ready and willing to submit, even to death, if that was God's will. Daniel was willing to do *anything* God required of him to facilitate the release of his people. Daniel's loyalty to God is extraordinary and God's approval of Daniel is amazing. In fact, Daniel's loyalty became the very tool that God used to glorify His name before the Medes and Persians so that He could deliver the Jews from captivity! If the plot to kill Daniel was clever, God's use of the situation was even more so. God used the administrator's hatred of Daniel, Darius' affection for Daniel, and Daniel's loyalty (and ultimately the lion's den) to set Israel free from slavery. Watch how these elements combined to accomplish God's plan.

King Darius Humiliated

The next morning, "**. . . the king gave the order, and they brought Daniel and threw him into the lions' den. The king said to Daniel, 'May your God, whom you serve continually, rescue you!' A stone was brought and placed over the mouth of the den, and the king sealed it with his own signet ring and with the rings of his nobles, so that Daniel's situation might not be changed. Then the king returned to his palace and spent the night without eating and without any entertainment being brought to him. And he could not sleep.**" (Daniel 6:16-18)

Daniel was arraigned before King Darius. When the king saw the old prophet in sackcloth and ashes, he became furious with his administrators. He saw through their plot. Daniel, "the Jew," was no rebel and Darius knew that. In fact, Daniel was the only administrator the king could trust! According to law, however, Daniel was subjected to the usual "loyalty" interrogation and without hesitation, confessed to praying to his God three times a day. Daniel did not offer excuses, plead his case or beg for his life. Even more importantly, he did not swear an oath of loyalty to King Darius as his highest authority. King Darius churned with grief. He condemned himself all night for failing to consider the intense hatred of his administrators for Daniel, "the Jew." How ironic the twist of events. Darius was planning to promote Daniel, but now he would have to kill him instead. Darius knew Daniel was unjustly condemned, but not even the king himself could change the law of the Medes and Persians. With these words, "**May your God, whom you serve continually, rescue you!**" Darius bids farewell to Daniel. The king gives the order and with his own ring and the rings of those who hated the old Jew, seals Daniel's fate to be thrown into the lion's den. Daniel was at peace, Darius was in torment, and the administrators were on their way to a secret celebration party.

King Darius Exhilarated

"**At the first light of dawn, the king got up and hurried to the lions' den. When he came near the den, he called to Daniel in an anguished voice, 'Daniel, servant of the living God, has your God, whom you serve continually, been able to rescue you from the lions?' Daniel answered, 'O king, live forever! My God sent his angel, and he shut the mouths of the lions. They have not hurt me, because I was found innocent in his sight. Nor have I ever done any wrong before you, O king.' The king was overjoyed and gave orders to lift Daniel out of the den. And when Daniel was lifted from the den, no wound was found on him, because he had trusted in his God. At the king's command, the men who had falsely accused Daniel were brought in and thrown into the lions' den, along with their wives and children. And before they reached the floor of the den, the lions overpowered them and crushed all their bones. Then King Darius wrote to all the peoples, nations and men of every language throughout the land: 'May you prosper greatly! I issue a decree that in every part of my kingdom people must fear and reverence the God of Daniel. For he is the living God and he endures forever; his kingdom will not be destroyed, his dominion will never end. He rescues and he saves; he** performs signs and wonders in the heavens and on the Earth. He has rescued Daniel from the power of the lions.' So Daniel prospered during the reign of Darius [the Mede] and the reign of Cyrus the Persian." (Daniel 6:19-28, insertion mine) Thoughtfully consider the profound experience of Darius that morning. Upon hearing Daniel's voice, a pagan king was given every reason that morning to put his faith in the God of Daniel. The tomb was opened and "a dead man" was received by the living! The king immediately published another decree requiring every person in his kingdom to fear and reverence the God of Daniel, "the Jew." The news about Daniel's miraculous deliverance was told everywhere! Only when you consider the Chaldeans intense hatred for the Jews does the significance of Darius' actions stand out. Because of Daniel's loyalty, the God of Heaven was exalted to the highest position through the eyes and lips of a heathen king. This demonstrates an interesting point that all religious people would do well to remember. The objective of serving the God of Heaven is to bring honor and glory to God, not to self.

Israel Set Free

The story of Daniel's miraculous deliverance and the immediate destruction of his enemies by the *same* lions that refused to eat him has been closely examined for some important reasons. First, remember that God's timing is *always* perfect! Evidently, the lion's den episode happened during Darius' first calendar year, 538/7 B.C. This allowed time for Darius to become acquainted with Daniel and to develop such confidence in him that he wanted to make him the number two man in his kingdom. As we are about to see, the timing of the lion's den event was also perfect!

God used the hatred of the administrators and the loyalty of Daniel in a way that no one could have anticipated. I believe the events unfolded as follows: When Daniel sought the Lord in sackcloth and ashes for instructions on what he should do to facilitate the deliverance of Israel, God heard Daniel's prayer and gave Daniel something that Daniel did not know he was about to need. God gave Daniel *peace* in the face of death. This peace is reflected in Daniel's courageous action after he learned about the law. God did not give Daniel wisdom to outfox the evil administrators, nor did God rain down plagues on Babylon like He did in Egypt. God had a better plan in mind.

After Daniel violated man's law, God honored Daniel's loyalty to His law with protection and enormous notoriety. (No one had ever spent a night in a den of wild and ravenous lions and lived to tell about it.) Simultaneously, God eliminated a big obstacle that stood in the way of delivering His people. God granted Darius a *legal* opportunity to purge his government of men who had proven their disloyalty to the interests of the king. Politically speaking, the death of these administrators would make the release of the Jews a manageable problem for the king, even though Darius did not know the Jews were about to be set free. After Darius destroyed the administrators who hated Daniel, the king promoted Daniel to the number two position in his kingdom and no one else complained!

Evidently, King Darius died the following year after the lion's den event and King Cyrus absorbed the territory of Darius into his expanding kingdom. Therefore, the ascension year of Cyrus over the province of Babylon was 537/6 B.C. and his first calendar year was 536/5 B.C. Because of Daniel's notoriety from the lion's den event and because he was the highest official in Darius' kingdom, Daniel became well acquainted with King Cyrus during his ascension year. During the Spring of 536/5 B.C., which was the 70th year of captivity, King Cyrus met with Daniel. Daniel informed the Persian king that the God of Heaven had chosen him to be a great king before he was even born. Daniel showed King Cyrus the writings of the prophet Isaiah where Cyrus is called *by name* in Scripture years before Cyrus was born. (Isaiah 45:1-4) When Daniel explained to King Cyrus why he was fasting and praying – the behavior that ultimately sent him to the lion's den – the king's heart was moved at the loyalty and devotion of this elderly man to the Supreme God over Heaven and Earth. Daniel informed Cyrus that the God of Heaven had appointed the Persian king to set the Jews free, "without price or reward," (Isaiah 45:13) for the purpose of rebuilding His temple. This same God of Heaven had delivered Daniel from the lion's den and the rest of the story is history. Cyrus issued the decree in Daniel's presence in the 70th year, a Friday year, in the Spring of 536 B.C. The Bible says, **"In the first year of Cyrus king of Persia, in order to fulfill the word of the Lord spoken by Jeremiah, the Lord moved the heart of Cyrus king of Persia to make a proclamation throughout his realm and to put it in writing: 'This is what Cyrus king of Persia says: "The Lord, the God of heaven, has given me all the kingdoms of the earth and he has appointed me to build a temple for him at Jerusalem in Judah. Anyone of his people among you— may his God be with him, and let him go up to Jerusalem in Judah and build the temple of the Lord, the God of Israel, the God who is in Jerusalem." ' "** (Ezra 1:1-3) The timing could not have been more perfect. The decree of Cyrus ended 70 years of captivity (counting inclusively). It is amazing how God took one loyal man through the lion's den so that Daniel could present the will of God to a king who now controlled the province of Babylon, as well as the territory of Judea! This decree was possible because Cyrus ruled over the province of Babylon where the Jews were captives, as well as the territory of Judea where Jerusalem was located. The greatest problem was solved. God's timing is so perfect. His ways are so magnificent! Remember, God required the release of slaves during the Friday year (the sixth year) and this is exactly what He did for the nation of Israel. The decree of Cyrus occurred in 536 B.C., a Friday year.

> **Note:** The Bible does not indicate that Darius died in 537/6 B.C. For two reasons, this point is deduced from the course of events recorded in Daniel 6 and Daniel 9. First, even though they are contemporary kings, Darius and Cyrus did not rule over Daniel or the province of Babylon at the same time. Second, history says that Cyrus had been a Persian king for more than 20 years before his *first* year over the province of Babylon came about. In order for Cyrus to become king over the province of Babylon, death had to eliminate Darius from the throne in 537 B.C. If this is a

correct assumption, Cyrus' ascension year over Babylon is 537/6
B.C. and Cyrus' first calendar year is 536/5 B.C. The Bible
confirms this scenario by saying, **"So Daniel prospered during
the reign of Darius and the reign of Cyrus the Persian."**
(Daniel 6:28) This text can be understood from the perspective
that Daniel prospered during the reign of Darius which was
followed by the reign of Cyrus. Of course, this text can also be
interpreted to mean that Daniel prospered during the co-regent
reign of both kings, but it seems evident that both kings did not
rule over Daniel or the province of Babylon at the same time.
Other facts may come to light in the future that offers a better
answer. Ancient history aside, the good news is that we know the
70 years were fulfilled in a timely way. The Bible says, **"The land
enjoyed its Sabbath rests; all the time of its desolation it
rested, until the seventy years were completed in fulfillment of the word of the Lord spoken by Jeremiah."**
(2 Chronicles 36:21)

Calendar of Events

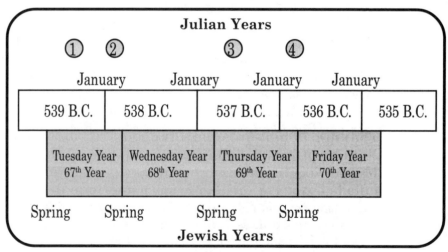

1. **Babylon falls, ascension year for Darius**
2. **First year for Darius, lion's den**
3. **Darius dies, ascension year for Cyrus**
4. **First year for Cyrus, frees the Jews**

End Time Parallels

As we see how God used the loyalty test to set His people free, it is easy to compare the parallels of the Great Tribulation. Here are some parallels for you to consider: Revelation 13:8 says, **"All inhabitants of the Earth will worship the beast – all whose names have not been written in the book of life belonging to the Lamb that was slain from the creation of the world."** This text implies that false worship will become a matter of law during the Great Tribulation because all of the world will not voluntarily worship the beast. In other words, when the world is *squeezed* by threats of severe punishment, "all inhabitants of the Earth" will worship the beast, except those who have a higher loyalty to the worship of God. The human race is about to be squeezed very hard. That ancient serpent, the devil, the roaring lion from the lion's den, is about to make war upon the saints. (Revelation 12:17) Revelation 13 predicts the devil will wage war upon the saints for 42 months using tCircumstances can *squeeze* us to a point that our highest loyalties are revealed. he force and penalty of laws. (Revelation 13:5) The end result is that the saints will be *legally* persecuted! **"He** [the Antichrist] **was given power** [from God] **to give breath** [life] **to the image of the first beast** [the one-world-church-state which the devil will set up], **so that it could speak** [decree laws] **and cause all who refused to worship the image to be killed. He also forced everyone, small and great, rich and poor, free and slave, to receive a** [visible] **mark on his right hand or on his forehead, so that no one could buy or sell unless he had the mark, which is the name of the beast or the number of his name."** (Revelation 13:15-17, insertions mine) There it is! The coming loyalty test will boil down to survival. Those people who are loyal and worship God will be hunted down as criminals and shut off from the necessities of life. The saints will be forced to live by faith in God because they will not be able to obtain the necessities of life. However, those people who have the highest loyalty for personal survival will submit to the mark of the beast, a tattoo that will be placed on the forehead or the right hand. Officials in their devil's government will wear the devil's name tattooed on the foreheads. (This is a counterfeit of what God intends to do to the 144,000. They will wear the name of Jesus and the Father on their foreheads throughout eternity. See Revelation 14:1.) Ordinary citizens will wear the literal number, 666, tattooed on their right hand. Billions of people will submit to wearing a tattoo that they know is evil in order to survive. This test will prove where our highest loyalties are!

Another parallel between Daniel's experience and the Great Tribulation is timing. Just as God set His people free right on time, God will set the saints free from the curse of sin – right on time. Several prophecies of Daniel and Revelation tell us there are important time-periods during the Great Tribulation. God has predetermined the number of days and we know His timing is perfect!

There are many more end time parallels between Daniel and his lion's den experience and the Great Tribulation. I have mentioned a few to encourage you to practice putting the Lord first in your life. I encourage you to seek the Lord through prayer and fasting. For the past two years WUAS supporters have been fasting and praying on the seventh day of each month. Why don't you join us? We want God to use us in whatever way possible to share the good news of the coming King of kings. We pray for the outpouring of Holy Spirit power. We want to be sure that we are willing to do anything that God asks of us. If Daniel had been lax about his loyalty to God, when the test came he would have fumbled, faltered and failed. Loyalty to God does not suddenly spring up when the consequence for disobedience against the law of the land is death. Loyalty to God is a way of life that requires practice and determination. Webster describes loyalty as being constant and faithful, bearing true allegiance. What Webster did not know is that the highest loyalty of every human being is about to be revealed!

Chapter 2
A Faith More Precious Than Gold

In Chapter 1, we studied the experience of Daniel in the lion's den and how God used Daniel's faith to set His people free from their Babylonian captivity. Now, I would like to share a story that explains why God put Daniel's three friends in a fiery furnace. I want to share these stories of faith because they have so much to say about the coming drama predicted in Revelation. As you proceed through this story, see if you can detect any end time parallels.

God's Agent of Wrath

King Nebuchadnezzar set siege to Jerusalem three times. He finally destroyed the city in 586 B.C. because Israel refused to submit to his "higher" authority. Even though the secular mind might say that Jerusalem was destroyed because of rebellion against Nebuchadnezzar, the Bible indicates that Jerusalem was destroyed because Israel refused to submit to God's authority. (See Jeremiah 25 and Ezekiel 14.) The destruction of Israel by Nebuchadnezzar teaches a profound truth: God's longsuffering and wrath against Israel are but a mirror reflecting how God deals with all nations. (Leviticus 18:28; Jeremiah 25:12; Acts 10:34) God preserved a biblical record of His actions so future generations could understand why "*He* sets up governments and takes them down." In this particular story, understand that God selected Nebuchadnezzar to be His servant; His agent of wrath against Israel. (Jeremiah 25:9; 27:6; 43:10) In other words, God empowered and enabled the king of the North, Nebuchadnezzar, to destroy His city and His people because of their decadence. (Daniel 9) The role of Nebuchadnezzar, as the king from the North and as the king of Babylon, parallels the coming of the

Antichrist. During the Tribulation, Lucifer will be the "stern-faced king" from the north (Daniel 8:23; 11:36) and also the king of modern Babylon! (Revelation 17:11) This is just the beginning of end time parallels.

Three Sins

God's patience with Israel ended because of three persistent sins: Israel violated His Sabbaths, engaged in sexual immorality and preferred to worship idols instead of Almighty God. (Do you see an end time parallel in this?) Thoughtfully consider the words of God as He laments the apostasy of Israel: **"Her priests do violence to my law and profane my holy things; they do not distinguish between the holy and the common; they teach that there is no difference between the unclean and the clean; and they shut their eyes to the keeping of my Sabbaths, so that I am profaned among them."** (Ezekiel 22:26, insertion mine)

Also consider God's comments about the clergy of Israel: **" 'And among the prophets of Jerusalem I have seen something horrible: They commit adultery and live a lie. They strengthen the hands of evildoers, so that no one turns from his wickedness. They are all like Sodom to me; the people of Jerusalem are like Gomorrah . . . For they have done outrageous things in Israel; they have committed adultery with their neighbors' wives and in my name have spoken lies, which I did not tell them to do. I know it and am a witness to it,' declares the Lord."** (Jeremiah 23:14; 29:23) **"Therefore this is what the Sovereign Lord says: 'I myself am against you, Jerusalem, and I will inflict punishment on you in the sight of the nations. Because of all your detestable idols, I will do to you what I have never done before and will never do again. Therefore in your midst fathers will eat their children, and children will eat their fathers. I will inflict punishment on you and will scatter all your survivors to the winds.' "** (Ezekiel 5:8-10)

We learn from Isaiah, Jeremiah and Ezekiel why God's anger with Israel reached a boiling point. His holy name had been profaned among the nations of Earth by Israel's decadence. As representatives of the Most High God and trustees of the everlasting gospel, Israel's rebellion had degenerated them to such a decadent condition that God could no longer use Israel for the benefit of the world. Destruction was the only solution. Therefore, God Himself chose a "servant-destroyer," the king of Babylon, to destroy His original plan, His city and His people.

The Vanished Vision

Daniel and his three friends, Shadrach, Meshach and Abednego, were taken to Babylon as prisoners of war during the first siege of Nebuchadnezzar in 605 B.C. Shortly after they arrived, God exalted Daniel and his friends before King Nebuchadnezzar through a curious turn of events. One night God gave Nebuchadnezzar a vision that outlined the remaining course of human history. (Daniel 2) Essentially, the vision consisted of a great statue of a man that was made out of various materials. At the end of the vision, the statue was smashed to pieces by a great rock that came out of the sky. When the king awoke, he became agitated for two reasons. First, Nebuchadnezzar knew that he had received an important vision, but he could not remember what it was. He initially thought it was from Marduk, the god of the Babylonians. Second, as the king fretted over his loss of memory, he realized that he had no other option but to ask the clergy of Babylon for help. The king did not have complete confidence in the "wise men" of Babylon and he anticipated a skirmish with them. To stop this before it started, Nebuchadnezzar made it clear that he would not tolerate any delay or double talk on their part.

Behind the scenes, the God of Heaven was unfolding a plan to exalt His holy name throughout the world. Nebuchadnezzar's vision was from the God of Heaven, not Marduk, and it was the God of Heaven who gave the king amnesia. By doing this, God made fools of Babylon's clergy and at the same time, revealed the impotence of Marduk. Even though the vanished vision agitated the king, the agitation caused by that vanished vision became the very means through which young Daniel became exalted to a position close to the king.

God Is So Clever

After rising from bed and I am sure, pacing the floor, Nebuchadnezzar called an emergency meeting for all the wise men of the palace. Suspecting lame excuses and weasel words, Nebuchadnezzar confronted his wise men with these words: **"So the king summoned the magicians, enchanters, sorcerers and astrologers to tell him what he had dreamed. When they came in and stood before the king, he said to them, 'I have had a dream that troubles me and I want to know what it means.' Then the astrologers answered the king in Aramaic, 'O king, live forever! Tell your servants the dream, and we will interpret it.' The king replied to the astrologers, 'This is what I have firmly decided: If you do not tell me what my dream was and interpret it, I will have you cut into pieces and your houses turned into piles of rubble. But if you tell me the dream and explain it, you will receive from me gifts and rewards and great honor. So tell me the dream and interpret it for me.' Once more they replied, 'Let the king tell his servants the dream, and we will interpret it.' Then the king answered, 'I am certain that you are trying to gain time** [so that you can create another one of your incoherent riddles], **because you realize that this is what I have firmly decided: If you do not** [immediately] **tell me the dream, there is just one penalty for you.** [If you do not tell me the dream, I will know that] **You have conspired to tell me misleading and wicked things** [during times past]**, hoping the situation will** [favorably] **change** [in each instance to fit your predictions]. **So then** [since you claim to have contact with the god of Babylon]**, tell me the dream, and I will know** [beyond doubt] **that you can interpret it for me.' "** (Daniel 2:2-9, insertions mine)

Nebuchadnezzar was no dummy. Consider his speech to the wise men. If the wise men proved to be a bunch of clever liars, he would destroy them. If they really did have a supernatural connection with Marduk, *as they had claimed*, they would be rewarded. The astrologers, magicians, sorcerers and enchanters represented Babylon's diverse religion and they claimed, from time to time, to have received visions from Marduk on behalf of the king. *Their claims of contact with Marduk almost led to their demise.*

False Prophets

In ancient times, kings often sought the services of religious leaders as counselors and advisors. For example, Jezebel employed 450 prophets of Baal. (1 Kings 18:19) Even as late as the fourth century A.D., Constantine depended heavily upon the advice and flattery of the theologian, Eusebius. Clergymen were sometimes deemed important because rulers believed that their prosperity depended on staying within the favor of "the gods." To earn their "salt," religious leaders had to walk a fine line. They had to be very careful with their words. They not only had to say things that bolstered the ego of their employer, they had to say things in a way that could not be proven false. For this reason, "wise men" were notoriously hard to "pin down." They always had an "out" hidden somewhere in their riddles and prophecies.

In ancient times, the highest rank among the clergymen was that of a prophet. (Remember Balaam? See Numbers 22.) Any person who had direct connection with "the gods" was highly honored, respected and paid well. It is ironic that God's prophets in Israel had just the opposite fate. They were often stoned or executed because Israel's kings did not want to hear the truth! (Matthew 23:37) In most cases, to become a "prophet," all a person had to do was claim that he or she had received a message from one of "the gods." Of course, a prophet was validated when his prophecy came to pass, but this was the point that bothered Nebuchadnezzar. Babylon's prophets presented their messages with such slippery words that they always seemed to come true, no matter how the situation unfolded. However, when Daniel stood before the king and repeated the vision and declared its interpretation, the king immediately recognized the veracity of Daniel's words. Daniel was a "true" prophet speaking clearly and decisively. He did not use weasel words! Therefore, Nebuchadnezzar promptly promoted Daniel above all the prophets in Babylon.

Let me explain one thing. A false prophet is a person who claims to speak for God when God has not spoken to that person. As Israel degenerated, she became full of false prophets and this made God very angry. Prophets were saying "God showed this to me," or "God said this to me," when in fact God had said nothing or showed nothing. The reason this makes God so angry is because it is only a matter of time until His Word is defamed and considered worthless because of prophetic falsehoods. God feels so strongly about this that He promises to destroy anyone who uses His name for the sake of credibility, when in reality a false prophet is speaking out of his own imagination. (See Ezekiel 13.) Lucifer is called the "false prophet" in Revelation 19:20 for this very reason. He will speak out of his own evil imagination, claiming to be God!

So, in an effort to stay within the king's favor (and earn their keep), Babylon's prophets made up fables and riddles to please and flatter the king. But Nebuchadnezzar was smart enough to know that (a) a dream cannot be validated or studied by other people, and (b) although a false prophet can say that he or she has received a vision, no one can prove otherwise if the message cannot be clearly nailed down. (See also 1 Kings 18:22 and 2 Kings 3.) So, when Nebuchadnezzar demanded the wise men to reveal the vanished vision, he turned the tables on them. There was no room to deceive. The king reasoned that if his wise men really had contact with Marduk, if they received visions as he had, and if they had the ability to interpret visions from Marduk, then they *should be* able to determine, describe, and interpret the vision which Marduk gave the king. So, the king was ready to confront his "wise men" and frame his request in a way that left no wiggle room. When the wise men considered the demand of the king, they knew they were in big trouble. They would not be able to weasel their way out of this confrontation. Consider their defense: **"The astrologers answered the king, 'There is not a man on earth who can do what the king asks! No king, however great and mighty, has ever asked such a thing of any magician or enchanter or astrologer. What the king asks is too difficult. No one can reveal it to the king except the gods, and they do not live among men.' This made the king so angry and furious that he ordered the execution of all the wise men of Babylon."** (Daniel 2:10-12) Can you imagine being summoned to the palace for an emergency meeting only to discover that your execution is minutes away? In the presence of Nebuchadnezzar, all of the wise men of Babylon were forced to admit deceit and failure. How clever of the God of Heaven to have the wise men confess with their own mouths the impotence of the Babylonian religion. When the moment of truth came, the clergy of Babylon were disgraced and the king was justifiably furious with them.

Marduk Is No God

Before God would exalt His holy name throughout the Earth, He chose to demonstrate that Marduk was "no god." It is amazing how a vanished dream turned the world of the religious leaders upside down. Before the vision took place, the prophets of Babylon were highly paid and widely respected as "wise men." After meeting with the king for only a few minutes, the "wise men" of Babylon confirmed with their own mouths that they were just "a clutch of liars" with a death sentence hanging over their heads. I am reminded of Paul's words, **"But God chose the foolish things of the world to shame the wise; God chose the weak things of the world to shame the strong."** (1 Corinthians 1:27) Do you see an end time parallel here? (Hint: Is it possible that few, if any, of the 144,000 will be theologians?)

Remember, the ultimate point of this story is that God wanted to vindicate His holy name before the nations of Earth. He wanted the whole world to know that He was a God of love and salvation, a God of mercy and justice, a God of fairness and truth, a God of compassion and majesty. Unfortunately, just the opposite had occurred. The Jews had made enemies of almost everyone on Earth. They had slandered and profaned the exalted name of God, trampled upon His law, and rejected every prophet He sent to them. So, God implemented a plan to restore His good name and He chose to use the mouth of a heathen king to do it! A sovereign God can make a servant out of anyone or anything.

The Death Decree

News of a sudden and unexpected death decree for all the wise men of Babylon flew from the palace of Nebuchadnezzar as fast as a horse can go. The "news media" was on this story in a heartbeat. The threat of death for all the wise men of Babylon did something that Nebuchadnezzar would later regret. The king had unwittingly informed the whole world of the impotence of Babylon's wise men by putting a death decree on their heads. Even worse, the entire kingdom became eager to know the contents of the vision that had vanished, and they wondered what was so imperative about the vision that the king would kill all of his wise men.

Daniel Exalted

Through a series of providential events, Daniel eventually stood before the king. He not only revealed the vanished vision, but he also interpreted the vision for the king. This pleased the king more than words can express. When the king heard Daniel's testimony, he was thrilled: **"Then King Nebuchadnezzar fell prostrate before Daniel and paid him honor and ordered that an offering and incense be presented to him. The king said to Daniel, 'Surely your God is the God of gods and the Lord of kings and a revealer of mysteries, for you were able to reveal this mystery.'**

Then the king placed Daniel in a high position and lavished many gifts on him. He made him ruler over the entire province of Babylon and placed him in charge of all its wise men." (Daniel 2:46-48)

A few hours later, after pondering the consequences of his rash decisions, the king had a change of heart. He must have grimaced as he faced three sobering truths: First, Daniel had informed the king that Marduk did not give him the vision. Nebuchadnezzar's vision came from the Most High God *of the Jews,* those despicable people. They were the lowest class of people in Nebuchadnezzar's kingdom and he did not want to admit that they had a God greater than the Babylonians. Second, Daniel told the king that the God of the Jews was sovereign over all the kingdoms of the world, even Babylon. Nebuchadnezzar heard how God sets up kings and takes them down, according to His sovereign authority. Nebuchadnezzar was flattered to learn that it was the God of Heaven who had given *him* a throne. At the time, the reality of Daniel's words had not sunk in. God wanted Nebuchadnezzar to know that he had not gained the throne by human prowess, but this lesson would not be learned until the king was humbled and spent seven years living as an animal. The third truth was the most chilling of all. God told the king that *his* kingdom would fall and it would be destroyed in days to come. As the king churned on the vanished vision and the train of events that it produced, he must have thought his vision was more of a nightmare than a revelation from God.

The King Distressed

Nebuchadnezzar's impatience with the wise men had created a political nightmare. The king had publically humiliated and discredited the wise men of Babylon. He had tested the god of the Babylonians and proved that Marduk was inferior to the God of the Hebrews. Worst of all, he had fueled the curiosity of his subjects by putting a death decree on the heads of Babylon's wise men. Everyone wanted to know the contents of the vanished vision! The seriousness of a death decree for Babylon's religious leaders indicated this vision was not a trivial matter. Furthermore, when the Jewish teenager, Daniel, was promoted above all the wise men of Babylon, it was obvious to everyone that Daniel had successfully recalled and interpreted the vision for the king. So, the vision had been recalled and interpreted, but what did it say?

We know the vision predicted the fall of Babylon and other world empires, but Nebuchadnezzar did not want his subjects to know that the God of the Hebrews had predestined the fall and destruction of his empire. The king knew that if this information leaked out, his government would collapse. A government cannot survive without the submission and loyalty of its subjects. If the news of Babylon's predestined fall reached the ears of his top administrators, Nebuchadnezzar knew he would soon be a king without a throne. How could anyone maintain confidence in a king that was predestined to destruction by the Most High God? Nebuchadnezzar realized that a long tenure on the throne was only possible for as long as people *were loyal* to him and his regime. If his subjects knew that God had numbered his days, they would rise up in rebellion and he would perish.

Kings may conquer nations and kings may kill thousands to secure their authority, but no king can thwart the God of Heaven. The rumor began to spread that the fall of Babylon was predestined by the God of the Jews. Based on Nebuchadnezzar's subsequent actions, I believe it is safe to conclude that the administrators from the far reaches of the empire must have sent requests for clarification so that they could deal with the rumors about the vision. As the situation worsened, Nebuchadnezzar consulted with his embarrassed wise men and they decided to dissolve the rumor by mixing error with truth. Nebuchadnezzar chose to distort the truth that was given to him in the vision for a number of practical and political purposes. The wise men owed their lives to the king (actually to Daniel and his three friends) because the king relented on the death decree. Consequently, they were very eager to help the king solve his political problem. Nebuchadnezzar and his wise men conspired to tell the world that Marduk had given the king a great vision of a "golden man." The people would be told that the golden man represented the kingdom of Babylon, *which would last forever.* Based on the course of events, Nebuchadnezzar evidently alleged to his subjects that he "was commanded" in vision to empty the golden coffers of Babylon to erect a great golden replica of his vision. Because the rumor had circulated that Babylon was predestined to fall, the king decided to use the golden image as a way to renew loyalty to his government. He planned to require all of his administrators and governors to travel to the province of Babylon so that they might be present on the day when the vision of the "golden image" would be told by the king and the image dedicated.

The construction of a 90-foot tall golden image of a man began in earnest. (It is believed that a cubit in ancient Babylon equaled 18-20 inches, so 60 cubits [in height] would equal about 90 feet. For comparison's sake, the Statue of Liberty is 111 feet tall, but Lady Liberty stands on a pedestal that is 194 feet high, which makes her total height 305 feet.) Due to the swiftness of rumors and the irreparable damage they could cause, there was no time for delay. Riders on horses were dispatched to the ends of the Earth calling the administrators and governors to be present on the Plain of Dura at an appointed time. Nebuchadnezzar anticipated some resistence to his plans, so he ordered the giant smelting furnaces that were used to cast the metal man to be kept burning during the dedication service. The loyalty test would be "real simple." If anyone refused to bow down and worship the golden image, they would be thrown into a furnace. The king calculated his loyalty test would <u>force</u> everyone back into "the fold" if any loyalties had been compromised by the rumor that Babylon was destined for destruction. The immediate death of rebels would reduce potential problems. The king was satisfied that this course of action would protect his throne.

I Did It My Way

Now remember that Nebuchadnezzar believed that he had *earned* his throne through political savvy and military prowess. (Daniel 4:30) He heard, but did not comprehend the words of Daniel, indicating that his kingdom had been *given* to him by the God of Heaven. Therefore, the king thought a golden image and a loyalty test would bring an end to the rumor that Babylon was predestined to fall. It is possible that this is the most expensive lie ever told. Consider the amount of gold that was required to cast a statue 90 feet tall. Consider the amount of labor for making such an image and the amount of travel and logistics necessary to bring thousands of administrators from the farthest corners of the Earth to the Plain of Dura. This whole story highlights an interesting point about the carnal heart: Power can be of greater value than money. Men will go to extremes to gain or hold on to power. (We regularly see politicians spend millions to win a government office that pays very little money. Why do they do this?) To keep his lie covered up, Nebuchadnezzar prevented Daniel from attending the service. He had highly honored Daniel for telling the truth, but now that he was implementing a great lie, he did not want Daniel to be at the service to observe his foolishness.

A Time of Testing

When Daniel was promoted above the wise men of Babylon, Daniel asked that his friends be recognized for their contribution toward solving the mystery of the vanished vision. (Daniel 2:18,49) Their promotion almost proved to be the cause of their death. The king wanted everyone who was someone in his government to be present at the dedication of the golden image. In a political setting, the question of loyalty is paramount to everything else. *One man can exercise power over others only if the others are willing to submit.*

Daniel's friends, Meshach, Shadrach and Abednego, knew the test of loyalty was coming. What should they do? They could not run and hide because they had been given high positions in the government of Babylon by the king. Furthermore, the

impotent wise men of Babylon were jealously eager to have
Daniel and these "three Jews" removed from their high offices.
Therefore, if they were to avoid the dedication of the golden
image they would show reluctance in honoring the king. Hesitation on this point could be regarded as treason. As the date
approached, I am sure Daniel and his friends met together to
ask the Lord for divine intervention. On the basis of their
testimony during the dedication service, it is safe to say that
Shadrach, Meshach and Abednego obediently went to the
service expecting to be thrown into the fiery furnace. What
courage! But, this is exactly what God wanted! God needed
three young men who were willing to go to their death so that
He could exalt His holy name. Remember, this story began
when God wanted to correct the bad impression that the nation
of Israel had given of Him. The Jews had profaned His holy
name and God wanted to set the record straight. In order to do
this, God needed an expensive golden image, a pagan king who
knew the truth, a large crowd of world leaders who were
confused by rumors, a very hot fiery furnace and three young
men who would be faith-full unto death.

The Moment of Truth

**"So the satraps, prefects, governors, advisers, treasur-
ers, judges, magistrates and all the other provincial
officials assembled for the dedication of the image that
King Nebuchadnezzar had set up, and they stood before
it. Then the herald loudly proclaimed, 'This is what you
are commanded to do, O peoples, nations and men of
every language: As soon as you hear the sound of the
horn, flute, zither, lyre, harp, pipes and all kinds of
music, you must fall down and worship the image of
gold that King Nebuchadnezzar has set up. Whoever
does not fall down and worship will immediately be
thrown into a blazing furnace.' Therefore, as soon as
they heard the sound of the horn, flute, zither, lyre,
harp and all kinds of music, all the peoples, nations and
men of every language fell down and worshiped the
image of gold that King Nebuchadnezzar had set up. At**

this time some astrologers came forward and denounced the Jews." (Daniel 3:3-8)

All of a sudden, the dedication service stopped. As far as the eye could see, all but three Jews had bowed down before the golden man. The wise men wasted no time reporting this anomaly to the king. The three men were arrested and presented to the king. The golden image was forgotten. The music stopped. Everyone looked around to see what was about to happen. Every eye focused on three young Jews who dared to rebel against the monarch of Babylon! As they approached the throne of the king, the king must have uttered some bad Babylonian words under his breath, "How did *they* get here?" The king was embarrassed and frustrated. The whole dedication service could unravel and the result could be worse than the truth he was trying to hide!

Did you notice who reported the insolence of the three Hebrews? The wise men were the first to denounce the Jews. This is amazing. The wise men owed their very lives to these three young men and yet, the wise men were the first to report their disobedience to the king. (There is an end time parallel here.) **"They said to King Nebuchadnezzar, 'O king, live forever! You have issued a decree, O king, that everyone who hears the sound of the horn, flute, zither, lyre, harp, pipes and all kinds of music must fall down and worship the image of gold, and that whoever does not fall down and worship will be thrown into a blazing furnace. But there are some Jews whom you have set over the affairs of the province of Babylon – Shadrach, Meshach and Abednego – who pay no attention to you, O king. They neither serve your gods nor worship the image of gold you have set up.' Furious with** [embarrassment and] **rage, Nebuchadnezzar summoned Shadrach, Meshach and Abednego. So these men were brought before the king, and Nebuchadnezzar said to them, 'Is it true, Shadrach, Meshach and Abednego, that you do not serve my gods or worship the image of gold I have set up?' "** (Daniel 3:9-14, insertion mine)

The king personally knew Shadrach, Meshach and Abednego. He knew their integrity and loyalty. He knew they were close friends of Daniel, but somehow they had been overlooked. They should not be present. Now, he had no other option but to destroy them if he wanted to protect his throne. The king was "up the creek." Nebuchadnezzar, the king of Earth, had created a big lie, but the God of Heaven had gathered everyone together to hear and see the truth that was greater than Nebuchadnezzar's golden lie. (The truth of God is best seen when it is confronted with a great lie.) The king responded to the rebellion of Meshach, Shadrach and Abednego with feigned generosity, hoping they would humor him on this matter. The king had a big political problem on his hands (which he had created by threatening the wise men), and he knew he did not need a showdown with the Most High God of these three men. So the king tried to appear generous: **"Now when you hear the sound of the horn, flute, zither, lyre, harp, pipes and all kinds of music, if you are ready to fall down and worship the image I made, very good. But if you do not worship it, you will be thrown immediately into a blazing furnace. Then what god will be able to rescue you from my hand?"** (Daniel 3:15)

The words of Nebuchadnezzar are interesting. The king honestly knew these three lads were not rebellious toward him; after all, they had joined with Daniel in seeking an answer to his vanished vision. But the king was haughty enough to taunt the lads with the remark, **"Then what god will be able to rescue you from my hand?"** The king uttered these words because *he knew* of their loyalty to their God. He may have even known about the second commandment of their God. The action of the king reveals another interesting fact about the carnal heart: The performance of a miracle does not always change it. (Centuries later, Jesus raised Lazarus from the dead in the presence of many unbelievers and some of them still refused to accept Christ as the Messiah! See John 11.) In Nebuchadnezzar's case, the king had personally experienced the vanished vision and witnessed a second miracle when Daniel told him what he had dreamed. But neither event changed the king's heart. When confronted with their loyalty to the King of kings, the king of Earth thought he had the high ground, but as it turns out, he was on holy ground! To protect his lies, the king had to kill those who *stood* for the truth. He knew that they knew the truth about the vanished vision because he had promoted them. He also knew that he could never recover from public disgrace if he showed any sign of weakness or timidity in the presence of thousands of his administrators. So, the king did what every carnal heart would do and the young men did what every born-again believer would do. The metal in each heart was revealed.

"Shadrach, Meshach and Abednego replied to the king, 'O Nebuchadnezzar, we do not need to defend ourselves before you in this matter [because you know the truth and we know the truth about the vanished vision]. **If we are thrown into the blazing furnace, the God we serve is able to save us from it, and he will rescue us from your hand, O king. But even if he does not, we want you to know, O king, that we will not serve your gods or worship the image of gold you have set up.' "** (Daniel 3:16-18)

Shadrach, Meshach and Abednego had prepared for this moment. Through prayer and fasting, they had strengthened their resolve to stand firm for God. This event was a showdown between the gold of Babylon and the pure gold of faith in God. When the king saw that these young men were not going to acquiesce and "go along" with his plan, he became very angry. They had publically rejected his authority and this was the very thing he was trying to protect with the creation and dedication of the golden image!

"Then was Nebuchadnezzar full of fury, and the form of his visage was changed against Shadrach, Meshach, and Abednego: therefore he spake, and commanded that they should heat the furnace one seven times more than it was wont to be [normally] **heated. And he commanded the most mighty men that were in his army to bind**

Shadrach, Meshach, and Abednego, and to cast them into the burning fiery furnace. Then these men were bound in their coats, their hosen [trousers], and their hats, and their other garments, and were cast into the midst of the burning fiery furnace." (Daniel 3:19-21, KJV, insertions mine)

I used the KJV for these verses because I like the language. The Bible says "the form of his visage was changed." I understand this to mean that Nebuchadnezzar's face turned fiery red (maybe his blood pressure hit 220/160). He was hotter than a firecracker on the fourth of July because his kingly ego had been hammered. Here is a mystery: *Even though the carnal heart is full of rebellion, the carnal heart hates rebellion more than anything else.* When the carnal heart cannot get its way, its fury knows no limits. The king was rejected and no king or carnal heart can tolerate rebellion. Rejection or the fear of rejection is the underlying basis for peer pressure and a lot of social torment. To successfully deal with rejection, a person must receive daily injections of spiritual courage and stamina. Meshach, Shadrach and Abednego were at peace with their fate on that day because they had walked and talked with God. They had practiced obedience in small things – this was not their first test. This is a very important point. Loyalty that can withstand the prospect of a fiery death does not come overnight. Instead, it comes in little steps.

The God of Heaven Takes Over

"The king's command was so urgent and the furnace so hot that the flames of the fire killed the soldiers who took up Shadrach, Meshach and Abednego, and these three men, firmly tied, fell into the blazing furnace. Then King Nebuchadnezzar leaped to his feet in amazement and asked his advisers, 'Weren't there three men that we tied up and threw into the fire?' They replied, 'Certainly, O king.' He said, 'Look! I see four men walking around in the fire, unbound and unharmed, and the fourth looks like a son of the gods.' Nebuchadnezzar

then approached the opening of the blazing furnace and shouted, 'Shadrach, Meshach and Abednego, servants of the Most High God, come out! Come here!' So Shadrach, Meshach and Abednego came out of the fire, and the satraps, prefects, governors and royal advisers crowded around them. They saw that the fire had not harmed their bodies, nor was a hair of their heads singed; their robes were not scorched, and there was no smell of fire on them." (Daniel 3:22-27)

The death of Nebuchadnezzar's soldiers proved to the vast audience that the heat of the furnace was extreme. The soldiers who threw the three Jews into the furnace went to their death because they were loyal and obedient to their earthly king. The three Hebrews that were supposed to go to their death were obedient and loyal to their Heavenly King. (Exodus 20:4-6) In both cases, loyalty was present, but the greater question is: "Which king deserves highest loyalty?" While the three Hebrews were being bound and thrown into the furnace, the king's mind was in turmoil. He had to recover from the showdown caused by these three Jews. He watched with interest as the young men were bound and thrown into the furnace. As he observed their fate and his authority over their life, the king is surprised! Instead of seeing three bodies consumed by fire, he saw *four* men walking around in the furnace. The king jumped to his feet and asked, **"Weren't there three men that *we* tied up and threw into the fire?"** His attendants assured him this was the case. Then, the king exclaimed, **"Look! I see four men walking around in the fire. . . . "** Nebuchadnezzar immediately recognized this had to be the presence of God with the three Hebrews.

Nebuchadnezzar knew the golden image service was a charade. Nebuchadnezzar knew he was in the wrong when he sent Shadrach, Meshach and Abednego to the fiery furnace. In spite of knowing these things, the king followed a course of action that protected his material interests. He did this because his highest loyalties centered on himself. In this sense, Nebuchadnezzar demonstrated a carnal heart that plagues all of humankind. Nothing on Earth is more selfish and self-seeking than the carnal heart. The root of the world's problems today is selfishness.

"Then Nebuchadnezzar said, 'Praise be to the God of Shadrach, Meshach and Abednego, who has sent his angel and rescued his servants! They trusted in him and defied the king's command and were willing to give up their lives rather than serve or worship any god except their own God. Therefore I decree that the people of any nation or language who say anything against the God of Shadrach, Meshach and Abednego be cut into pieces and their houses be turned into piles of rubble, for no other god can save in this way.' Then the king promoted Shadrach, Meshach and Abednego in the province of Babylon." (Daniel 8:29-30)

What does a humiliated king say to an enormous gathering of world governors when his death decree upon three Jews was made null and void by a miracle? The king did not admit defeat, nor did the king offer an apology to the God of the Heaven. Instead, he turned to his impotent wise men and confused administrators and said, "If any of you speak evil about the God of Shadrach, Meshach and Abednego, you will be cut in pieces!" Wow! The king deflects his responsibility once again. The carnal heart of the king rejected another chance to be transformed. Later, the God of Heaven finally got the king's attention by exiling him to the field as an animal for seven years – but that's another story.

The End of This Story

When the administrators and governors returned to their distant homes, they had a story to tell! In a few words their story went like this, "Yes, we saw the golden man, but let me tell you about the God of the Jews. He delivered three young men out of a roaring fiery furnace. We saw it with our own eyes. The fire was so hot it killed the king's soldiers, but the flames did not hurt those three Jews! That is some God the Jews have." This story, repeated by a thousand pagans all over the world, exalted the God of Heaven. As a nation, the Jews had profaned the wonderful name of God, but God found three Jews who had a faith of pure gold and He was able to exalt His holy name through their obedience and loyalty.

There are many important end time parallels in this story. During the end time, there will be an "image to the beast" and all people will be required to worship it or be killed. (Revelation 13) You and I will be players in the drama that is forthcoming. It is possible that we may have to stand before the dreaded king of Babylon (Lucifer). Will we have a faith of pure gold? **"To the angel of the church in Laodicea write: These are the words of the Amen, the faithful and true witness, the ruler of God's creation. I know your deeds, that you are neither cold nor hot. I wish you were either one or the other! So, because you are lukewarm – neither hot nor cold – I am about to spit you out of my mouth. You say, 'I am rich; I have acquired wealth and do not need a thing.' But you do not realize that you are wretched, pitiful, poor, blind and naked. I counsel you to buy from me gold refined in the fire, so you can become rich; and white clothes to wear, so you can cover your shameful nakedness; and salve to put on your eyes, so you can see. Those whom I love I rebuke and discipline. So be earnest, and repent. Here I am! I stand at the door and knock. If anyone hears my voice and opens the door, I will come in and eat with him, and he with me. To him who overcomes, I will give the right to sit with me on my throne, just as I overcame and sat down with my Father on his throne. He who has an ear, let him hear what the Spirit says to the churches."** (Revelation 3:14-22)

Chapter 3

Esther – Beautiful Savior

The Bible is the most amazing book on Earth and it takes time and effort to get acquainted with its treasures. Pure gold and precious gems do not lay on the surface of the ground and neither do the riches of God's grace lie on the surface of the pages in the Bible. Patient and persistent effort must come first, before the precious nuggets of truth are discovered.

In this chapter, I would like to share another dramatic Bible story that has important end time parallels for your consideration. It is the story of how God used two beautiful women, Vashti and Esther, to rescue His people. God included this story in the Bible for several reasons, and I would like to share some insights about their story that fascinate me. This story begins in 483 B.C., during the third year of King Xerxes. I have modified the biblical narrative in the Book of Esther in several places for clarity and brevity. Comments in [brackets or italics] are my insertions.

Part I – Vashti Says "No" [Biblical Narrative]

[King] Xerxes ruled over 127 provinces stretching from India to Cush [Egypt]. [He] reigned from his royal throne in the citadel of Susa, and in the third year of his reign he gave a banquet for all his nobles and officials. The military leaders of Persia and Media, the princes, and the nobles of the provinces were present. For a full 180 days he displayed the vast wealth of his kingdom and the splendor and glory of his majesty. When these days were over, the king gave a banquet, lasting seven days . . . for all the people from the least to the greatest, who were in the citadel of Susa . . . . Wine was served in goblets of gold, each one different from the other, and the royal wine was abundant, in keeping with the king's liberality. . . .

[Simultaneously] Queen Vashti hosted a banquet for the [women of Susa] in the royal palace of King Xerxes. On the seventh day, when King Xerxes was in high spirits from wine, he commanded the seven eunuchs who served him . . . to bring Queen Vashti, wearing her royal crown, in order to display her beauty to the people and nobles, for she was lovely to look upon. But when the attendants delivered the king's command, Queen Vashti refused to come. Then the king became furious and burned with anger. Since it was customary for the king to consult experts in matters of law and justice, he spoke with the wise men who understood the [protocols and laws of the day] . . . "According to law, what must be done to Queen Vashti?" he asked. "She has not obeyed the command of King Xerxes that the eunuchs have taken to her. Then [one of the wise men] Memucan replied in the presence of the king and the nobles, "Queen Vashti has done wrong, not only against the king but also against all the nobles and the peoples of all the provinces of King Xerxes. For the queen's conduct will become known to all the women [throughout the kingdom because many women are with her at the feast next door], and they will despise their husbands and say, 'King Xerxes commanded Queen Vashti to be brought before him, but she would not come.' This very day the Persian and Median women of the nobility who have heard about the queen's conduct will respond to all the king's nobles in the same way. There will be no end of disrespect and discord [toward men]. Therefore, if it pleases the king, let him issue a royal decree and let it be written in the laws of Persia and Media, which cannot be repealed, that Vashti is never again to enter the presence of King Xerxes. Also, let the king give her royal position to someone else who is better than she. Then when the king's edict is proclaimed throughout all his vast realm, all the women will respect their husbands, from the least to the greatest." The king and his [less than sober] nobles were pleased with this advice, so the king did as Memucan proposed. He sent dispatches to all parts of the kingdom, to each province in its own script and to each people in its own language, proclaiming in each people's tongue that every man *should be* ruler over his own household." (Taken from Esther 1)

Comments

When Vashti was summoned to the banquet room, she knew the king and all his friends were drunk because they had been partying for seven days. She instinctively knew that to parade before a bunch of drunken men was a recipe for trouble. Vashti was well aware of her beauty and the influence it had on men. Evidently the king wanted a sensual display of beauty. She knew that if one drunk fool made a suggestive remark about her in the king's presence, the hilarity and high spirit of this grand occasion could suddenly turn into an ugly brawl of rage and violence. She was trapped in a very difficult situation because the women of the kingdom looked to her as an example of what they should do. She rightly chose to refuse the invitation of the king, even though she knew it would cost her dearly. Contrast the different parties: The king was drinking, feasting, and having a jolly good time. The queen, on the other hand, was in her chamber on the verge of tears.

It would be an understatement to say that King Xerxes was highly embarrassed by his wife's refusal. Each time I read this part of the story I laugh out loud. I can picture a befuddled king consulting with his befuddled advisors – all of them trying to figure out what to do with a woman who just said "No." Judging by the conversation, their biggest fear was that Vashti's example would encourage all of the women in the kingdom to just say "No," to their husband's demands. How ironic that these mighty men of valor are fearful that there will be no end to trouble from women. So, they concoct a plan that is supposed to keep all women in submission. Their advice, inflamed by drunkenness, prompted the king to make a great proclamation in many different languages. In short, the decree said: "Women must obey their husbands." What is so amusing

about this situation is that the drunken king issues a decree to
127 provinces that even he cannot fulfill. Xerxes ruled over
much of the then known world. He had power over life and
death, but he could not control his wife. (I do not think there is
an end time parallel in this part of the story – I am still smil-
ing.) Even though Vashti wisely refused her husband's command, she was not physically harmed. Perhaps the Lord
protected her from the usual punishment issued for defiance.
However, Vashti's refusal did set a sequence of events in
motion that eventually propelled a beautiful Jewish girl to
Xerxes' side as Queen of the Medes and Persians! Actually,
the hand of God caused this episode of musical-chairs. It was
God's purpose to move Vashti off the throne and let Esther
replace her on the throne because a sinister event was about to
unfold.

Part II – Esther Made Queen [Biblical Narrative]

[About three years] later when the anger of King Xerxes had
subsided, he remembered Vashti and what she had done and
what he had decreed about her. Then the king's personal
attendants proposed, "Let a search be made for beautiful
young virgins for the king. Let the king appoint commissioners
in every province of his realm to bring all these beautiful girls
into the harem at the citadel of Susa." . . . Now there was in
the citadel of Susa a Jew of the tribe of Benjamin, named
Mordecai son of Jair. . . . Mordecai had a [young female] cousin
named Hadassah, whom he had brought up because she had
neither father nor mother. This girl, who was also known as
Esther, was lovely in form and features, and Mordecai had
taken her as his own daughter when her father and mother
died. When the king's order and edict had been proclaimed,
many girls [including Esther] were brought to the citadel of
Susa and put under the care of Hegai . . . who had charge of
the harem. [Esther] pleased him and won his favor. Immediately he provided her with beauty treatments and special food.
He assigned to her seven maids selected from the king's palace
and moved her and her maids into the best place in the harem.

Esther had not revealed her nationality and family background, because Mordecai had forbidden her to do so. . . .
Esther was taken to King Xerxes in the royal residence in the
tenth month, the month of Tebeth, in the seventh year of his
reign. Now the king was attracted to Esther more than to any
of the other women, and she won his favor and approval more
than any of the other virgins. So he set a royal crown on her
head and made her queen instead of Vashti. And the king gave
a great banquet, Esther's banquet, for all his nobles and officials. He proclaimed a holiday throughout the provinces and
distributed gifts with royal liberality. (Taken from Esther 2)

Part III – Haman Loathes Mordecai [Biblical Narrative]

[A few weeks after Esther's banquet, Uncle] Mordecai was
sitting at the king's gate [when], Bigthana and Teresh, two of
the king's officers who guarded the doorway, became angry and
conspired to assassinate King Xerxes. But Mordecai found out
about the plot and told Queen Esther, who in turn reported it
to the king, giving credit to Mordecai. And when the report
was investigated and found to be true, the two officials were
hanged on a gallows. All this was recorded in the book of the
annals in the presence of the king. . . .

[Months later] King Xerxes decided to honor [his best friend, a
very wealthy man named] Haman . . . elevating him and
giving him a seat of honor higher than that of all the other
nobles. All the royal officials at the king's gate knelt down and
paid honor to Haman, for the king had commanded this concerning him. But Mordecai would not kneel down or pay him
honor. Then the royal officials at the king's gate asked
Mordecai, "Why do you disobey the king's command?" Day
after day they spoke to him but he refused to comply. Therefore they told Haman about it to see whether Mordecai's behavior would be tolerated, for he had told them he was a Jew.
When Haman saw that Mordecai would not kneel down or pay
him honor, he was enraged. Yet having learned who Mordecai's
people were, he scorned the idea of killing only Mordecai [for

Haman and all of the nobles hated the Jews]. Instead, Haman
looked for a way to destroy all Mordecai's people, the Jews,
throughout the whole kingdom of Xerxes." (Taken from Esther
2 and 3)

Part IV – A Universal Death Decree Approved [Biblical Narrative]

[About five years after Esther became queen] "In the twelfth
year of King Xerxes, in the first month, the month of Nisan,
they cast the pur (that is, the lot – see note on the following
page) in the presence of Haman to select a day and month [to
kill all of the Jews]. And the lot fell on the twelfth month, the
month of Adar. Then Haman said to King Xerxes [cleverly,
without mentioning the word "Jew"], "There is a certain people
dispersed and scattered among the peoples in all the provinces
of your kingdom whose customs are different from those of all
other people and who do not obey the king's laws; it is not in
the king's best interest to tolerate them. If it pleases the king,
let a decree be issued to destroy them, and I will put ten thousand talents of silver [about 375 tons!] into the royal treasury
for the men who carry out this business." So the king took his
signet ring from his finger and gave it to Haman . . . the
enemy of the Jews. "Keep the money," the king said to Haman,
"and do with these people as you please . . . " Then on the
thirteenth day of the first month the royal secretaries were
summoned. They wrote out in the script of each province and
in the language of each people all Haman's orders . . . and
sealed it with [the king's] own ring. Dispatches were sent by
couriers to all the king's provinces with the order to destroy,
kill and annihilate all the Jews – young and old, women and
little children – **on a single day, the thirteenth day of the
twelfth month**, the month of Adar [February/March], and to
plunder their goods. A copy of the text of the edict was to be
issued as law in every province and made known to the people
of every nationality so they would be ready for that day.
Spurred on by the king's command, the couriers went out, and
the edict was issued in the citadel of Susa. The king and

Haman sat down to drink, but the city of Susa was bewildered.
(Taken from Esther 3)

> **Note:** The casting of the pur (or lots) was an ancient method for
> determining the will of God. The casting of the pur was more
> than a casual or random decision. For example, we toss a coin at
> the beginning of a football game to determine who will possess
> the football. The casting of the pur was considered more serious.
> Gentiles (like Haman and the sailors that cast Jonah overboard –
> Jonah 1:7), as well as the Jews, used the pur because they
> believed it revealed the will of God. For example, on the Day of
> Atonement, the pur was cast in the presence of the Lord to
> determine which goat would be the Lord's goat. (Leviticus 16:8)
> When Israel entered the promised land, the pur was cast in the
> presence of the Lord to determine how the land would be divided
> among seven of the twelve tribes. (Joshua 18:1-10) Even the
> Romans cast the pur to divide up the clothing of Jesus. (Matthew
> 27:35) The interesting point here is that the **thirteenth day of
> the twelfth month** was set by the casting of the pur. Because
> each month begins with a new moon in God's calendar, it is
> possible for the thirteenth day of the month to be a full moon.
> (Due to elliptical orbit of the moon, a full moon can occur as early
> as the thirteenth day and as late as the fifteenth day of a
> month.) Having the light of a full moon to finish off the Jews
> must have been a definite plus in Haman's wicked mind when he
> saw the results. As it turns out, the Jews were able to use the
> light of a full moon to finish off their enemies. As you will see,
> there is more to the date and timing of the universal death
> decree issued on God's people and it was more than just a ran-
> dom event.

Part V – Esther's Test [Biblical Narrative]

When Mordecai learned of all that had been done, he tore his
clothes, put on sackcloth and ashes, and went out into the city,
wailing loudly and bitterly. But he went only as far as the
king's gate, because no one clothed in sackcloth was allowed to
enter it. . . . Then Esther summoned Hathach, one of the king's
eunuchs assigned to attend her, and ordered him to find out
what was troubling Mordecai and why. So Hathach went out
to Mordecai in the open square of the city in front of the king's

gate. Mordecai told him everything that had happened to him, including the exact amount of money Haman had promised to pay into the royal treasury for the destruction of the Jews. He also gave him a copy of the text of the edict for their annihilation, which had been published in Susa, to show to Esther and explain it to her, and he told [Hathach] to urge her to go into the king's presence to beg for mercy and plead with him for her people.

Hathach went back and reported to Esther what Mordecai had said. Then she instructed him to say to Mordecai, "All the king's officials and the people of the royal provinces know that for any man or woman who approaches the king in the inner court without being summoned the king has but one law: that he be put to death. The only exception to this is for the king to extend the gold scepter to him and spare his life. But thirty days have passed since I was called to go to the king." When Esther's words were reported to Mordecai, he sent back this answer: "Do not think that because you are in the king's house you alone of all the Jews will escape. For if you remain silent at this time, relief and deliverance for the Jews will arise from another place, but you and your father's family will perish. And who knows but that you have come to royal position for such a time as this?" Then Esther sent this reply to Mordecai: "Go, gather together all the Jews who are in Susa, and fast for me. Do not eat or drink for three days, night or day. I and my maids will fast as you do. When this is done, I will go to the king, even though it is against the law. And if I perish, I perish." (Taken from Esther 4)

Commentary

Queen Esther, like Queen Vashti before her, found herself in a very distressing situation. Even though she was *the* queen, the king had young concubines constantly clamoring for his attention. His emotional attachment to Esther was not like that of a typical husband and wife. She had not seen the king for a month when Mordecai implored her to go before him and plead for their lives! Esther knew that if she imposed herself upon the king by violating court protocol, she would likely die or face the same banishment as Vashti. She also knew that the law of the Medes and Persians, once made, could not be changed. As a female, she also knew that if she appeared too aggressive, the king might be repulsed. Esther had not forgotten Vashti's experience. These facts motivated her reluctant response to her uncle.

Mordecai responded to Esther with some very sober words: **"Do not think that because you are in the king's house you alone of all the Jews will escape. For if you remain silent at this time, relief and deliverance for the Jews will arise from another place, but you and your father's family will perish. And who knows but that you have come to royal position for such a time as this?"** This statement shows how great Mordecai's faith in God really was. He knew that if Esther refused, she too would perish because the law of the Medes and Persians showed no favoritism. Still, Mordecai encouraged her by saying that relief and deliverance for the Jews would arise from another place. Mordecai sincerely believed that God would not allow His people to become extinct at this time. Mordecai knew how God had promised Abraham that Messiah would come through his offspring and since Messiah had not appeared, Mordecai was 100% sure that God would deliver His people. The decree sent out by Haman, bearing the name of King Xerxes, was actually a universal death decree. It left no way out – every Jew was to be killed. Period.

Part VI – Esther's Banquet #1 [Biblical Narrative]

"On the third day [of fasting] Esther put on her royal robes and stood in the inner court of the palace, in front of the king's hall. The king was sitting on his royal throne in the hall, facing the entrance. When he saw queen Esther standing in the court, he was pleased with her and held out to her the gold scepter that was in his hand. So Esther approached and touched the tip of the scepter. Then the king asked, "What is it, Queen Esther? What is your request? Even up to half the kingdom, it will be given you." "If it pleases the king," replied Esther, "let the king, together with Haman, come today to a banquet I have prepared for him." "Bring Haman at once," the king said, "so that we may do what Esther asks." So the king and Haman went to the banquet Esther had prepared. As they were drinking wine, the king again asked Esther, "Now what is your petition? It will be given you. And what is your request? Even up to half the kingdom, it will be granted." Esther replied, "My petition and my request is this: If the king regards me with favor and if it pleases the king to grant my petition and fulfill my request, let the king and Haman come tomorrow to the banquet I will prepare for them. Then I will answer the king's questions." (Taken from Esther 5)

Commentary

The timing of these matters is beyond coincidence. For the sake of discussion, let us suppose the first banquet takes place on Monday evening. The king and Haman are present for very different reasons. The king is full of curiosity, and Haman, his best friend, is full of ego. The king knows something is up with his lovely Esther because no one would dare to approach him as Esther did unless there was a serious problem troubling her. Esther is timid and nervous and to get her to divulge what is on her heart, the king generously offers her anything she wants – up to half his kingdom!

Evidently, Esther sensed the mood that evening was not right for her request. So, she stalled by asking for another banquet – the following night. If this stalling technique was planned from the beginning, it surely worked. The king left the banquet more puzzled than before, and of course, Haman was only too pleased to attend another banquet. What greater honor could he hope for than to be seen dining with the king and queen once again?

Part VII – Haman Frustrated, The Sleepless King [Biblical Narrative]

Haman went out [from the banquet] happy and in high spirits. But when he saw Mordecai at the king's gate and observed that he neither rose nor showed fear in his presence, he was filled with rage against Mordecai. Nevertheless, Haman restrained himself and went home. Calling together his friends and Zeresh, his wife, Haman boasted to them about his vast wealth, his many sons, and all the ways the king had honored him and how he had elevated him above the other nobles and officials. "And that's not all," Haman added. "I'm the *only* person queen Esther invited to accompany the king to the banquet she gave. And she has invited me along with the king tomorrow. But all this gives me no satisfaction as long as I see that Jew Mordecai sitting at the king's gate." His wife Zeresh and all his friends said to him, "Have a gallows built, seventy-five feet high, and ask the king in the morning to have Mordecai hanged on it. Then go with the king to the dinner and be happy." This suggestion delighted Haman, and he had the gallows built.

[Meanwhile] That [same] night the king could not sleep; so he ordered the book of the chronicles, the record of his reign, to be brought in and read to him. It was found recorded there that Mordecai had exposed Bigthana and Teresh, two of the king's officers who guarded the doorway, who had conspired to assassinate King Xerxes. "What honor and recognition has Mordecai received for this?" the king asked. "Nothing has been done for him," his attendants answered.

[The next morning] The king said, "Who is in the court?" Now Haman had just entered the outer court of the palace to speak to the king about hanging Mordecai on the gallows he had erected for him. His attendants answered, "Haman is standing in the court." "Bring him in," the king ordered. When Haman entered, the king [without giving Haman a chance to speak] asked him, "What should be done for the man the king delights to honor?" Now Haman thought to himself, "Who is there that the king would rather honor than me?" So he answered the king, "For the man the king delights to honor, have them bring a royal robe the king has worn and a horse the king has ridden, one with a royal crest placed on its head. Then let the robe and horse be entrusted to one of the king's most noble princes. Let them robe the man the king delights to honor, and lead him on the horse through the city streets, proclaiming before him, 'This is what is done for the man the king delights to honor!' "

"Go at once," the king commanded Haman. "Get the robe and the horse and do just as you have suggested for Mordecai the Jew, who sits at the king's gate. Do not neglect anything you have recommended." So Haman got the robe and the horse. He robed Mordecai, and led him on horseback through the city streets, proclaiming before him, "This is what is done for the man the king delights to honor!" Afterward Mordecai returned to the king's gate. But Haman rushed home, with his head covered in grief, and told Zeresh his wife and all his friends everything that had happened to him. His advisers and his wife Zeresh said to him, "Since Mordecai, before whom your downfall has started, is of Jewish origin, you cannot stand against him – you will surely come to ruin!" While they were still talking with him, the king's eunuchs arrived and hurried Haman away to the banquet Esther had prepared. (Taken from Esther 6)

Commentary

Do you sense that the timing of these events cannot be coincidental? The *same* night that Haman decided to hang Mordecai, the king could not sleep, which led to the discovery that Mordecai's faithfulness had gone unrewarded! The next morning, Haman stops by the palace seeking permission to hang Mordecai while the king is searching for a way to highly honor the same Jew who Haman wants to kill! The king knows nothing about Haman's plans and Haman knows nothing of the king's desire! What are the odds of this happening? Imagine how Haman must have felt escorting Mordecai on a royal horse around Susa for a couple hours crying out, **"This is what is done for the man the king delights to honor!"** Haman's country club buddies must have split their sides in laughter when they saw this. How do you think Mordecai must have felt as he watched Haman lead the horse he was sitting on? Do you think a smile crossed his face?

Zeresh, Haman's wife, was insightful. She saw the fate of her proud husband immediately. Perhaps the Holy Spirit caused an utterance to come out of her mouth similar to the utterance that came out of Balaam's mouth when he tried to curse Israel. She said, **"Since Mordecai, before whom your downfall has started, is of Jewish origin, you cannot stand against him – you will surely come to ruin."**

History reveals that the Babylonians, the Medes and Persians, the Grecians, and the Romans all intensely disliked the Jews, as a nation of people. Even though relations between Israel and the Medes and Persians were never good, and even though relations between Israel and God were not as good as they should have been, God did not allow the nation of Israel to perish until He had fulfilled His promise to Abraham. After Jesus' ministry on Earth was finished, God permitted the Romans to destroy Jerusalem in A.D. 70.

Part VIII – Esther's Banquet #2 [Biblical Narrative]

So the king and Haman went to dine with Queen Esther, and as they were drinking wine on that second day, the king again asked, "Queen Esther, what is your petition? It will be given you. What is your request? Even up to half the kingdom, it will be granted." Then Queen Esther answered, "If I have found favor with you, O king, and if it pleases your majesty, grant me my life – this is my petition. And spare my people – this is my request. For I and my people have been sold for destruction and slaughter and annihilation. If we had merely been sold as

male and female slaves, I would have kept quiet, because no
such distress would justify disturbing the king." King Xerxes
asked Queen Esther, "Who is he? Where is the man who has
dared to do such a thing?" Esther said, "The adversary and
enemy [of the Jews] is this vile Haman." Then Haman was
terrified before the king and queen. The king got up in a rage,
left his wine and went out into the palace garden. But Haman,
realizing that the king had already decided his fate, stayed
behind to beg Queen Esther for his life.

Just as the king returned from the palace garden to the banquet hall, Haman was falling on the couch where Esther was
reclining. The king exclaimed, "Will he even molest the queen
while she is with me in the house?" As soon as the word left
the king's mouth, [fear] covered Haman's face. Then Harbona,
one of the eunuchs attending the king said, "A gallows seventy-
five feet high stands by Haman's house. He had it made for
Mordecai [this morning], who spoke up to help the king." The
king said, "Hang him on it!" So they hanged Haman on the
gallows he had prepared for Mordecai. Then the king's fury
subsided. That same day King Xerxes gave Queen Esther the
estate of Haman, the enemy of the Jews. And Mordecai came
into the presence of the king, for Esther had told how he was
related to her. (Taken from Esther 7 and 8)

Part IX – Justice Served [Biblical Narrative]

[Later, Esther went again before the king without permission.]
Esther again pleaded with the king, falling at his feet and
weeping. She begged him to put an end to the evil plan of
Haman [which the force of law]. . . . Then the king extended
the gold scepter to Esther and she arose and stood before him.
"If it pleases the king," she said, "and if he regards me with
favor and thinks it the right thing to do, and if he is pleased
with me, let an order be written overruling the dispatches that
Haman . . . devised and wrote to destroy the Jews in all the
king's provinces. For how can I bear to see disaster fall on my
people? How can I bear to see the destruction of my family?"

King Xerxes replied to Queen Esther and to Mordecai the Jew, "Because Haman attacked the Jews, I have given his estate to Esther, and they have hanged him on the gallows. Now write another decree in the king's name in behalf of the Jews as seems best to you, and seal it with the king's signet ring – for no document written in the king's name and sealed with his ring can be revoked.

At once the royal secretaries were summoned – on the twenty-third day of the third month, the month of Sivan. They wrote out all Mordecai's orders to the Jews, and to the satraps, governors and nobles of the 127 provinces stretching from India to Cush [Egypt]. These orders were written in the script of each province and the language of each people and also to the Jews in their own script and language. Mordecai wrote in the name of King Xerxes, sealed the dispatches with the king's signet ring, and sent them by mounted couriers, who rode fast horses especially bred for the king. The king's edict granted the Jews in every city the right to assemble and protect themselves; to destroy, kill and annihilate any armed force of any nationality or province that might attack them and their women and children; and to plunder the property of their enemies.

The day appointed for the Jews to do this in all the provinces of King Xerxes was **the thirteenth day of the twelfth month,** the month of Adar. A copy of the text of the edict was to be issued as law in every province and made known to the people of every nationality so that the Jews would be ready on that day to avenge themselves on their enemies. The couriers, riding the royal horses, raced out, spurred on by the king's command. And the edict was also issued in the citadel of Susa. Mordecai left the king's presence wearing royal garments of blue and white, a large crown of gold and a purple robe of fine linen. And the [Jews in the] city of Susa held a joyous celebration. For the Jews it was a time of happiness and joy, gladness and honor." (Taken from Esther 8)

Part X – Revenge [Biblical Narrative]

In every province and in every city, wherever the edict of the king went, there was joy and gladness among the Jews, with feasting and celebrating. And many people of other nationalities became Jews because fear of the Jews had seized them. On the thirteenth day of the twelfth month, the month of Adar, the edict commanded by the king was to be carried out. On this day the enemies of the Jews had hoped to overpower them, but now the tables were turned and the Jews got the upper hand over those who hated them. The Jews assembled in their cities in all the provinces of King Xerxes to attack those seeking their destruction. **No one could stand against them, because the people of all the other nationalities were afraid of them.** And all the nobles of the provinces, the satraps, the governors and the king's administrators helped the Jews, because **fear of Mordecai** had seized them. Mordecai was prominent in the palace; his reputation spread throughout the provinces, and he became more and more powerful. The Jews struck down all their enemies with the sword, killing and destroying them, and they did what they pleased to those who hated them.

In the citadel of Susa, the Jews killed and destroyed five hundred men. They also killed . . . the ten sons of Haman. . . . But they did not lay their hands on the plunder. The number of those slain in the citadel of Susa was reported to the king that same day. The king said to Queen Esther, "The Jews have killed and destroyed five hundred men and the ten sons of Haman in the citadel of Susa. What have they done in the rest of the king's provinces? Now what is your petition? It will be given you. What is your request? It will also be granted." "If it pleases the king," Esther answered, "give the Jews in Susa permission to carry out this day's edict tomorrow also [because revenge has not been fully accomplished], and let [the bodies of] Haman's ten sons be hanged on gallows." So the king commanded that this be done. An edict was issued in Susa, and they hanged the ten sons of Haman [in the public square to remind everyone of the penalty for mistreating the people of the queen].

The Jews in Susa came together on the fourteenth day of the month of Adar, and they put to death in Susa three hundred men, but they did not lay their hands on the plunder. Meanwhile, the remainder of the Jews who were in the king's provinces also assembled to protect themselves and get relief from their enemies. They killed seventy-five thousand of them but did not lay their hands on the plunder. This happened **on the thirteenth day of the month of Adar**, and on the fourteenth they rested and made it a day of feasting and joy. The Jews in Susa, however, had assembled **on the thirteenth and fourteenth**, and then on the fifteenth they rested and made it a day of feasting and joy. That is why rural Jews – those living in villages – observe the fourteenth of the month of Adar as a day of joy and feasting, a day for giving presents to each other. Mordecai recorded these events, and he sent letters to all the Jews throughout the provinces of King Xerxes, near and far, to have them celebrate **annually the fourteenth and fifteenth days of the month of Adar** as the time when the Jews got relief from their enemies, and as the month when their sorrow was turned into joy and their mourning into a day of celebration. **He wrote them to observe the days as days of feasting and joy and giving presents of food to one another and gifts to the poor.**

So the Jews agreed to continue the celebration they had begun, doing what Mordecai had written to them. For Haman, the enemy of all the Jews, had plotted against the Jews to destroy them and had cast the pur (that is, the lot) for their ruin and destruction. But when the plot came to the king's attention, he issued written orders that the evil scheme Haman had devised against the Jews should come back onto his own head, and that he and his sons should be hanged on the gallows. (Therefore these days were called Purim, from the word pur.) Because of everything written in this letter and because of what they had seen and what had happened to them, the Jews took it upon themselves to establish the custom that they and their descendants and all who join them should without fail observe these two days every year, in the way prescribed and at the time appointed." (Taken from Esther 9)

Comments

There are a few points in this story that have end time parallels. I would like to share five:

1. First, Esther's story illustrates how one clever man was able to set up a universal death decree for God's people. There is a direct end time parallel to this in Revelation 13 and Daniel 12. Revelation 13:15 says, **"He [the Antichrist] was given power to give breath to the image of the first beast, so that it could speak and cause all who refused to worship the image to be killed."** (Insertion mine.) This verse points forward to a time when a universal death decree will be set up for the saints. This death decree will occur during the Great Tribulation because God's people will refuse to worship the image of the beast (the one-world religion imposed by Lucifer), they will refuse the mark of the beast (the tattoo required by Lucifer), and they will refuse to submit to the laws of the Antichrist (Lucifer) who will be masquerading as God. Eventually, everyone (the saints) who refuse to obey the Antichrist will be condemned to death *at an appointed time.* Daniel tells us when the universal death decree occurs: **"From the time that the daily sacrifice is abolished and the abomination that causes desolation is set up, there will be 1,290 days. Blessed is the one who waits for and reaches the end of the 1,335 days."** (Daniel 12:11,12) There will be a death decree for the saints! God wants His children to know what is coming so they can stand firm in perilous times and have faith in His mighty arm of salvation. The story of Esther was put in the Bible for the purpose of building our faith. Bible prophecy indicates that the **daily** intercession of Jesus in Heaven's temple will come to a close, and this event will be marked by a global earthquake. (Revelation 8:2-5) When that occurs, the saints are to begin counting because 1,290 days later, a universal **death decree** will be "set up." Do not be afraid, because there is good news! The universal death decree will not be implemented because God, as He did in this story of Esther, will overturn the evil scheme of the Antichrist through a mighty display of power and authority.

2. The second end time parallel is this: In the story of Esther, God turned the universal death decree around so that the Jews could destroy their enemies without guilt! King Xerxes did not fret one bit that 75,800 people in his kingdom were killed. How marvelous are the ways of God. God created fear in the hearts of the Jews' enemies and they became powerless and easily defeated *at the appointed time*. This "fear element" needs some emphasis because this feature explains a profound point that is often overlooked in the Old Testament. When Israel was doing God's will, every battle was the Lord's battle, not theirs. Moses warned, "[If you love the Lord and serve him with all your heart] **Then all the peoples on earth will see that you are called by the name of the Lord, and they will fear you . . . . No man will be able to stand against you. The Lord your God, as he promised you, will put the terror and fear of you on the whole land, wherever you go.** " (Deuteronomy 28:10; 11:25, insertions mine) Israel was to be the arms and legs of God, and as long as Israel remained faithful to the Lord, the Bible says, **"The fear of God came upon all the kingdoms of the countries when they heard how the Lord had fought against the enemies of Israel."** (2 Chronicles 20:29) When Israel rebelled against the Lord, you guessed it, the enemies of Israel became bold and Israel became weak and afraid. Because a universal death decree was pronounced on Israel in Esther's day, the Jews became humble and submissive, and God honored their repentance. Did you notice in the story of Esther that many Gentiles became Jews because the fear of Jews was upon them? **". . . And many people of other nationalities became Jews because fear of the Jews had seized them."** (Esther 8:17) The same event will happen during the end time.

Many people will repent of their sins and become believers in Christ because they will see the power of God resting upon His people!

3. The third end time parallel is this: Mordecai recorded these events. **"He wrote them to observe the days** [of Purim] **as days of feasting and joy and giving presents of food to one another and gifts to the poor."** (Esther 9:22, insertions mine) This text is very interesting in light of the end time. To celebrate overwhelming victory over their enemies, the Jews were to perpetually observe the Feast of Purim with **"feasting and joy and giving presents of food to one another and gifts to the poor."** Now, compare Revelation 11:7-10: **"Now when they** [the Two Witnesses] **have finished their testimony, the beast that comes up from the Abyss** [Lucifer, the lamb-like beast] **will attack them, and overpower and kill them. . . . For three and a half days men from every people, tribe, language and nation will gaze on their bodies and refuse them burial. The inhabitants of the earth will gloat over them and will celebrate by sending each other gifts, because these two prophets had tormented those who live on the earth."** Especially notice the last sentence. The parallel between Purim and this event in Revelation is easy to see. A time is coming when the wicked will gloat and rejoice over the death of God's Two Witnesses because the Two Witnesses will be silenced. Basically, this text points forward to a time when Lucifer and his followers will gloat, rejoice and celebrate over the fact that God's work on Earth is brought to an end. Of course, this does not mean that God's plans or purposes have been destroyed. Yes, a time will come when the last of God's 144,000 messengers will be martyred and salvation is no longer offered. It is at that time when the torment of the Holy Spirit will cease. The wicked may gloat and rejoice because they think their torment is over, but that is not the end of the story.

4. The fourth end time parallel centers around the timing of the universal death decree in the Book of Esther. Remember, the date of the death decree in Esther's day was established by casting the pur. **"In the twelfth year of King Xerxes, in the first month, the month of Nisan, they cast the pur (that is, the lot) in the presence of Haman to select a day and month. And the lot fell on the twelfth month, the month of Adar. . . . Dispatches were sent by couriers to all the king's provinces with the order to destroy, kill and annihilate all the Jews – young and old, women and little children – on a single day, the thirteenth day of the twelfth month, the month of Adar, and to plunder their goods."** (Esther 3:7,13) I believe there is an amazing parallel between *the date* of the universal death decree in Esther's day and *the date* of the universal death decree during the Great Tribulation. In short, these two events appear to happen on the same day and in the same month, namely on a full moon in the month of Adar (February)!

5. The fifth end time parallel is found in the person of Esther. She represents Jesus, our lovely Savior in whom there is no defect. When Adam and Eve sinned, a universal death decree was placed upon the human race, but Jesus went before the King of the Universe. Through His intercession, we have been offered an escape from eternal death. Jesus was not only willing to die for His people, like Esther, but He also *did die* for you and me. Even though the Bible predicts a universal death decree will be set up for God's helpless people, it also says the saints have a Savior who is greater than the forces of evil. He will foil the wicked plans of Lucifer just like He did to Haman. He will turn the circumstances upside down, and God will impose the universal death decree on Satan and the armies of Earth. They will perish by the command (sword) that comes out of the mouth of Jesus at the Second Coming. I hope to see this with my own eyes! No wonder Daniel wrote, **"Blessed is the one who waits for and reaches the end of the 1,335 days."** (Daniel 12:12)

The story recorded in Esther tells us that God never sleeps and He always keeps vigil over His people. The story recorded in

Esther tells us that God's timing is always perfect, down to the split-second, when necessary. The story recorded in Esther tells us that God can turn a universal death decree into a glorious victory, if His children are faithful and loyal to Him. The story recorded in Esther points forward to a time when we, the last generation, will face the *same obstacles* that God's people faced some 2,500 years ago. I pray that each of us will be as faith-full as Mordecai and Esther. Their faith and courage show what God can accomplish *if* we are willing to stand up for what is right!

Chapter 4

Gideon – Reluctant Warrior

The book of Judges describes the first 350 years of Israel's experience in Canaan. The narrative begins during the time of Joshua (around 1398 B.C.) and ends just before Saul becomes Israel's king (around 1043 B.C.). During this period, the Lord Himself was Israel's King. Unfortunately, His people did not give Him much respect. In fact, the last verse in the book of Judges closes by saying, **"everyone did as he saw fit."** (Judges 21:25) After Joshua died, God called various men and women to be judges to guide and govern His wayward people, but they had limited success. Israel vacillated between submission to the Lord and rebellion against Him. Israel's inclination toward rebellion was a constant problem. In fact, the Bible suggests that there were seven periods of apostasy, seven periods of servitude and seven restorations during the time of the judges! God is changeless and the carnal nature is predictable. The history between God and Israel was preserved in the book of Judges for thousands of years and like a mirror, it reflects how He deals with all nations and people. In the same way, Israel's treatment of God reflects, like a mirror, how most of the human race treats God. *Actually, the Bible tells the story of our lives, only it uses different names!* If you and I had lived in those days, most of us would have fit right in with Israel's "on again" and "off again" relationship with the Lord! If God had destroyed Abraham's offspring at Mt. Sinai as He proposed to do (Exodus 32:10), and replaced Israel with the offspring of Moses, the results would have been the same – only the names would have changed. The Bible is an amazing book. It describes the present human condition with a thousand parallels from the past! When I study the Bible, I realize my own human nature is not that different from the antediluvians who scoffed as Noah built the ark. Sometimes, I am rebellious, like Israel. In some ways, I am blind, like the Pharisees. Other times, I am like the disciples and I do not understand the words of Jesus. In some ways, I am like doubting Thomas and impetuous Peter. When I am totally honest with myself, I realize that I have a lot in common with many Bible characters. In good ways and bad ways, they are like me and I am like them.

Two Nasty Problems

Seven cycles of "apostasy – servitude – restoration" in 350 years says much about the longsuffering of God, and also the inherent rebellion of humanity. Two problems plague the human race: Man's first and greatest problem is his innate rebellion against God's authority. The second problem is the ignorance between generations. On the topic of rebellion, we are spring-loaded from birth to reject everything that God wants of us. (Romans 8:7) For example, God insists that we rest on His Sabbath. I have yet to hear a person say when learning about God's Sabbath, "Wow! Look at the wonderful benefit God has set up for us! A day of rest each week. Yippee!" Actually, our hearts respond with just the opposite reaction. It typically goes like this: "Whoa! I don't know about this Sabbath rest thing. I have a job, family and friends, etc., to consider . . . ." Israel was no different and constantly struggled with their desire to abandon God's Sabbath rest! (Ezekiel 20) Truthfully, before you break any of God's commandments, you break the first commandment before any of the others! So, how is Israel's apostasy different from our apostasy? Refusing to obey God or justifying behavior that is contrary to God's commands is the same as Israel's rebellion. God knows that man's propensity toward rebellion can be moderated through punishment, just as a good parent disciplines a child. In fact, if we were truthful, almost everyone will give in and say "uncle" if tortured long enough.

During the time of the judges, Israel experienced God's judgments seven times and repented seven times, each time for the wrong reason! Have you ever heard someone say, "Lord, I will do anything you want, just answer my prayer"? This is the religious equivalent to saying "uncle." Again, this response indicates submission to God, but for the wrong reason. When suffering accomplishes its highest calling, suffering from God brings us into *humble* submission. We will pray as Jesus did when facing death, **"Father, if you are willing, take this cup from me; yet not my will, but yours be done."** (Luke 22:42)

Of course, God knew that the people of Israel repented because they experienced the hardships of His judgments. This is why God's punishments were redemptive for many centuries. God designed His wrath to bring the nation of Israel to her knees so that she might look up and consider the wisdom of her King. Good discipline may be punitive, but it should also be instructional! **"No discipline seems pleasant at the time, but painful. Later on, however, it produces a harvest of righteousness and peace for those who have been trained by it."** (Hebrews 12:11) Did you notice those last words, "for those who have been trained by it"? Some people are punished, yet they never get the point or learn the lesson. For example, more than 90% of certain classes of felons return to prison after being set free! In this case, discipline does not help if the lessons are not learned. This is why God has a second type of punishment called destructive punishment. When redemptive judgments fail, destructive judgments terminate the problem. For example, the world's inhabitants went beyond the point of redemption in Noah's day. If a worldwide, waist-deep flood could have achieved redemptive results, God would not have drowned the whole world and started over. God knew the cancer of sin and that redemption was out of the question, so He killed all but eight people and started over. God disciplined Israel with redemptive punishments for many centuries because He wanted Israel to wake up and observe the deadly consequences of sin. Eventually, God gave up and destroyed Israel as a nation in A.D. 70. God has a message for everyone on Earth about rebellion: Rebellion begins with forbidden pleasure or profit, which produces a harvest of sorrowful consequences and broken relationships. In the end, sin requires the penalty of death.

If we divide 350 years by seven "apostasy – servitude – restoration" cycles, the average is one cycle every 50 years (which is approximately once per generation). Since generations of people come and go, the second problem God has with humanity is the *"next* generation." A punished generation may repent and learn from God's discipline, but the *next* generation rarely reaps the benefits of discipline given to its elder generation! In fact, God has to start over with the *next* generation because it does not understand that God means what He says and is a powerful force. So, the younger generation arrives on the scene and makes the same mistakes as the previous generation and travels down a rebellious road, yielding to the temptations of sin. Then, the cycle of degeneration starts again. History constantly repeats itself because it is almost impossible for the *next* generation to possess the wisdom and experience of its elder generation! Therefore, the mistakes and the apostasy of former generations are repeated by the *next* generation.

God Keeps Vigil

With these thoughts in mind, I would like you to consider the story of Judge Gideon that includes several end time parallels. The story begins during one of Israel's suffering cycles – a time of servitude: **"Again the Israelites did evil in the eyes of the Lord, and for seven years he gave them into the hands of the Midianites. Because the power of Midian was so oppressive, the Israelites prepared shelters for themselves in mountain clefts, caves and strongholds. Whenever the Israelites planted their crops, the Midianites, Amalekites and other eastern peoples invaded the country. They camped on the land and ruined the crops all the way to Gaza and did not spare a living thing for Israel, neither sheep nor cattle nor donkeys. They came up with their livestock and their**

tents like swarms of locusts. It was impossible to count
the men and their camels; they invaded the land to
ravage it. Midian so impoverished the Israelites that
they cried out to the Lord for help." (Judges 6:1-6)

When the majority of people in a nation become decadent and
degenerate, the "Land-Lord of Earth" moves into action. God
hates sin and will destroy people who insist on rebellion. In
Israel's case, God gave His land over to the Midianites for
seven years. (If you want to know why the promised land is
"God's land" rather than Israel's land, see Leviticus 18:24,25;
25:23.) God made Israel's defenses weak and her borders
porous. Israel's "Homeland Defense Minister" could not stop
the terrorists from Midian from entering the land occupied by
Israel. The Midianites destroyed their homes, took their crops
and killed their animals. God allowed the Midianites to deci-
mate the promised land "that flowed with milk and honey"
because He was displeased with His people. **"When the
Israelites cried to the Lord because of Midian, he sent
them a prophet, who said, 'This is what the Lord, the
God of Israel, says: I brought you up out of Egypt, out of
the land of slavery. I snatched you from the power of
Egypt and from the hand of all your oppressors. I drove
them from before you and gave you their land. I said to
you, "I am the Lord your God; do not worship the gods
of the Amorites, in whose land you live." But you have
not listened to me.' "** (Judges 6:7-10) The words of the
prophet address the core problem. Israel had abandoned God
and His Sabbath rest and merged with mainstream religious
practices. Israel worshiped the hedonistic gods of the Amorites
(the Baals) because the Baals, unlike the God of Heaven, gave
people freedom to do whatever they wanted. Sexual immorality was not a controversial issue. In fact, it was considered
entertainment, a popular part of fertility cult worship. The
religion of the Baals was bewitching; a sensual religion that
appealed to the carnal passions of its worshipers.

Restoration

When the seven years of Midianite occupation had been
served, *God changed* Israel's desperate situation. Israel was
not allowed to weasel out of punishment. "They did the crime;
they did the time." The ironic point about this turn of events is
that God used the Midianites to punish Israel for their rebellion against Him, and then used Israel to destroy the
Midianites because of their great sexual immorality and de-
pravity! When the time came to set Israel free from Midianite
occupation, God chose the son of a prominent Baal worshiper
to be a Judge for Him. (Imagine that!) Gideon was a timid, but
sincere young man, who refused to worship the Baals. When
the story begins, Gideon (in his early 20's?) was threshing
wheat in his hideout. **"The angel of the Lord came and sat
down under the oak in Ophrah that belonged to Joash
the Abiezrite, where his son Gideon was threshing
wheat in a winepress to keep it from the Midianites.
When the angel of the Lord appeared to Gideon, he said,
'The Lord is with you, mighty warrior.' 'But sir,' Gideon
replied, 'if the Lord is with us, why has all this happened to us? Where are all his wonders that our fathers
told us about when they said, "Did not the Lord bring us
up out of Egypt?" But now the Lord has abandoned us
and put us into the hand of Midian.'**

[The Lord offered no explanation to Gideon why Israel was in
the hands of Midian. God had already explained this through
a prophet.]

**"The Lord turned to him and said, 'Go in the strength
you have and save Israel out of Midian's hand. Am I not
sending you?' 'But Lord,' Gideon asked, 'how can I save
Israel? My clan is the weakest in Manasseh, and I am
the least in my family.' The Lord answered, 'I will be
with you, and you will strike down all the Midianites
together.'**

"Gideon replied, 'If now I have found favor in your eyes, give me a sign that it is really you talking to me. Please do not go away until I come back and bring my offering and set it before you.' And the Lord said, 'I will wait until you return.' Gideon went in, prepared a young goat, and from an ephah of flour he made bread without yeast. Putting the meat in a basket and its broth in a pot, he brought them out and offered them to him under the oak. The angel of God said to him, 'Take the meat and the unleavened bread, place them on this rock, and pour out the broth.' And Gideon did so. With the tip of the staff that was in his hand, the angel of the Lord touched the meat and the unleavened bread. Fire flared from the rock, consuming the meat and the bread. And the angel of the Lord disappeared." (Judges 6:11-21)

These verses give me goose-bumps! I can just imagine Gideon running around, trying to get his offering together. Then, returning breathlessly, he puts the offering on a rock. The Lord stretches out His staff and "poof" – fire comes out of the rock and consumes the meat, bread – everything! The Lord suddenly disappears from view, but not from Gideon's presence!

"When Gideon realized that it was the angel of the Lord, he exclaimed, 'Ah, Sovereign Lord! I have seen the angel of the Lord face to face!' But the Lord said to him, 'Peace! Do not be afraid. You are not going to die.' So Gideon built an altar to the Lord there and called it The Lord is Peace . . . .

"That same night the Lord said to him, 'Take the second bull from your father's herd, the one seven years old. [Evidently, the first bull was their best breeding bull.] Tear down your father's altar to Baal and cut down the Asherah pole beside it. Then build a proper kind of altar to the Lord your God on the top of this height. Using the wood of the Asherah pole that you cut down, offer the second bull as a burnt offering.' So Gideon took ten of his servants and did as the Lord told him. But because *he was afraid of his family* and the men of the town, he did it at night rather than in the daytime.

"In the morning when the men of the town got up, there was Baal's altar, demolished, with the Asherah pole beside it cut down and the second bull sacrificed on the newly built altar! They asked each other, 'Who did this?' When they carefully investigated, they were told, 'Gideon son of Joash did it.' The men of the town demanded of Joash, 'Bring out your son. He must die, because he has broken down Baal's altar and cut down the Asherah pole beside it.' But Joash replied to the hostile crowd around him, 'Are you going to plead Baal's cause? Are you trying to save him? Whoever fights for him shall be put to death by morning! If Baal really is a god, he can defend himself when someone breaks down his altar.' So that day they called Gideon 'Jerub-Baal,' saying, 'Let Baal contend with him, because he broke down Baal's altar.' " (Judges 6:22-32, insertion and italics mine)

The Lord used this notable incident to let Israel know that He had chosen the young, timid Gideon as a leader. This action by Gideon was completely out of character! However, when God's Holy Spirit power rests on a willing heart, there is no limit to what God can accomplish! Gideon's father (a member of the elder generation) recognized the power of God upon his son and he successfully defended his son's behavior! (I believe Gideon's father's conscience condemned him in his heart for worshiping Baal.) God chose the weakest man in town to send a signal through the land that He was about to rescue His people. A few days later, this signal made perfect sense!

The Sword of the Lord and of Gideon

"Now all the Midianites, Amalekites and other eastern peoples joined forces and crossed over the Jordan and camped in the Valley of Jezreel. [They were intent on plundering the possessions of the Israelites.] **Then the Spirit of the Lord came upon Gideon, and he blew a trumpet, summoning the Abiezrites to follow him. He sent messengers throughout Manasseh, calling them to arms, and also into Asher, Zebulun and Naphtali, so that they too went up to meet them. Gideon said to God, 'If you will save Israel by my hand as you have promised – look, I will place a wool fleece on the threshing floor. If there is dew only on the fleece and all the ground is dry, then I will know that you will save Israel by my hand, as you said.' And that is what happened. Gideon rose early the next day; he squeezed the fleece and wrung out the dew – a bowlful of water.**

[The ever timid Gideon needs assurance, so he asks the Lord for a sign. God faithfully responds.]

"Then Gideon said to God, 'Do not be angry with me. Let me make just one more request. Allow me one more test with the fleece. This time make the fleece dry and the ground covered with dew.' That night God did so. Only the fleece was dry; all the ground was covered with dew.

[Again, the ever timid Gideon needs assurance. God patiently responds.]

"Early in the morning, Jerub-Baal (that is, Gideon) and all his men camped at the spring of Harod. The camp of Midian was north of them in the valley near the hill of Moreh. The Lord said to Gideon, 'You have too many men for me to deliver Midian into their hands. In order that Israel may not boast against me that her own strength has saved her, announce now to the people, "Anyone who trembles with fear may turn back and leave Mount Gilead."' So twenty-two thousand men left, while ten thousand remained.

[The ever timid Gideon begins to have heartburn. "Lord, too many soldiers?" How can an army ever have too many soldiers?]

"But the Lord said to Gideon, 'There are still too many men. Take them down to the water, and I will sift them for you there. If I say, "This one shall go with you," he shall go; but if I say, "This one shall not go with you," he shall not go.' So Gideon took the men down to the water. There the Lord told him, 'Separate those who lap the water with their tongues like a dog from those who kneel down to drink.' Three hundred men lapped with their hands to their mouths. All the rest got down on their knees to drink. The Lord said to Gideon, 'With the three hundred men that lapped I will save you and give the Midianites into your hands. Let all the other men go, each to his own place.' So Gideon sent the rest of the Israelites to their tents but kept the three hundred, who took over the provisions and trumpets of the others.

"Now the camp of Midian lay below him in the valley. During that night the Lord said to Gideon, 'Get up, go down against the camp, because I am going to give it into your hands. If you are afraid to attack, go down to the camp with your servant Purah and listen to what they are saying. Afterward, you will be encouraged to attack the camp.' So he and Purah his servant went down to the outposts of the camp.

[An ever timid Gideon needed more assurance. Notice how the Lord assures Gideon of victory over the Midianites and uses an enemy to confirm to Gideon what the Lord is going to do!]

"The Midianites, the Amalekites and all the other eastern peoples had settled in the valley, thick as locusts. Their camels could no more be counted than the sand on the seashore. Gideon arrived just as a man was telling a friend his dream. 'I had a dream,' he was saying. 'A round loaf of barley bread came tumbling into the Midianite camp. It struck the tent with such force that the tent overturned and collapsed.' His friend responded, 'This can be nothing other than the sword of Gideon son of Joash, the Israelite. God has given the Midianites and the whole camp into his hands.' When Gideon heard the dream and its interpretation, he worshiped God. He returned to the camp of Israel and called out, 'Get up! The Lord has given the Midianite camp into your hands.'

[The ever timid Gideon is now ready to lead 300 men into the camp of the Midianites.]

"Dividing the three hundred men into three companies, he placed trumpets and empty jars in the hands of all of them, with torches inside. 'Watch me,' he told them. 'Follow my lead. When I get to the edge of the camp, do exactly as I do. When I and all who are with me blow our trumpets, then from all around the camp blow yours and shout, "For the Lord and for Gideon." '

"Gideon and the hundred men with him reached the edge of the camp at the beginning of the middle watch [midnight], just after they had changed the guard. They blew their trumpets and broke the jars that were in their hands. The three companies blew the trumpets and smashed the jars. Grasping the torches in their left hands and holding in their right hands the trumpets they were to blow, they shouted, 'A sword for the Lord and for Gideon!'

"While each man held his position around the camp, all the Midianites ran, crying out as they fled. When the three hundred trumpets sounded, the Lord caused the men throughout the camp to turn on each other with their swords. The army fled to Beth Shittah toward Zererah as far as the border of Abel Meholah near Tabbath. Israelites from Naphtali, Asher and all

Manasseh were called out, and they pursued the Midianites. Gideon sent messengers throughout the hill country of Ephraim, saying, 'Come down against the Midianites and seize the waters of the Jordan ahead of them as far as Beth Barah.' So all the men of Ephraim were called out and they took the waters of the Jordan as far as Beth Barah. They also captured two of the Midianite leaders, Oreb and Zeeb. They killed Oreb at the rock of Oreb, and Zeeb at the winepress of Zeeb. They pursued the Midianites and brought the heads of Oreb and Zeeb to Gideon, who was by the Jordan." (Judges 6:33-7:25)

End Time Parallels

There are a few end time parallels in the story of Gideon to consider. Here are four:

1. The empowerment of Gideon and his army parallels the 144,000.

First, God chose a timid, self depreciating man. Then, God reduced Gideon's army to a mere 300 soldiers to eliminate any possibility for Gideon or the nation of Israel to claim victory over the Midianites. Similar circumstances will occur during the Great Tribulation. Contrary to what many people believe, God is not going to use a religious denomination to preach the gospel to the world. Instead, He will hand pick a few thousand people like Gideon. God's 144,000 servants will not be arrogant people, nor will they be influential scholars or great preachers. For the most part, they will be ordinary people. The victory they achieve will be the Lord's doing, not theirs! The ratio of God's servants to the population of the world will be about one per 50,000 people. God likes impossible odds. God will not share His glory with man. God is above man. God is omnipotent and He will show His strength through human weakness. **"But God chose the foolish things of the world to shame the wise; God chose the weak things of the** world to shame the strong. He chose the lowly things of this world and the despised things – and the things that are not – to nullify the things that are, so that no one may boast before him." (1 Corinthians 1:27-29)

2. God's wrath parallels the seven trumpets and the seven bowls.

God's punishment of Israel (seven years of occupation by the Midianites) was justified and God's destructive wrath toward the Midiantes was also justified! God gives every nation a measure of grace and a cup to measure iniquity. Grace runs out when the cup overflows with iniquity. When the majority of a nation's citizens conduct themselves in a way that is offensive to the "Lord of the Land," He moves into action. God's actions are redemptive at first. If they fail to accomplish redemption, God's judgments eventually become destructive. Historians may disagree with me, but I believe war is the handiwork of God. He uses one nation to destroy another when the offending nation fills its cup of iniquity. Then, if necessary, God destroys the destroyer if He deems it appropriate. Nations rise and fall – not by the prowess of man, but by divine decree. (See Daniel 5.)

God's wrath against Israel and the Midianites parallels the seven trumpets and the seven bowls of Revelation, respectively. The seven trumpets will be seven *first* plagues that have a generous measure of mercy mixed in. The seven trumpet judgments are redemptive judgments. This is why the quantity of "one-third" is mentioned twelve times during the seven trumpets. God spares two-thirds! The seven bowls are seven *last* plagues. These judgments have no mercy mixed in. God utterly destroys Earth and everyone on Earth (except the saints) by the time the events of the seventh bowl conclude. We see both types of judgments in the book of Judges. Israel received redemptive judgments and the Midianites received destructive judgments. (Eventually, Israel also received a destructive judgment as well.)

3. The confusion and defeat of the Midianites

Gideon and his army shattered the stillness of the night. Out of nowhere there came "a large army" with lights and trumpets. Generals in ancient times customarily directed their armies by the sound of "a" trumpet. The emphasis here on the word "a" is important. If there were many trumpets, no one would know which trumpet to follow. A soldier would hear multiple trumpets when various battalions converged on a battle. When the Midianites awoke to the sound of 300 trumpets, they had one thought. "We are out gunned and vastly out numbered!" Their resulting panic confirms this point.

When God's judgments (the seven trumpets) begin, the world will be taken by complete surprise. The world will awaken to a new reality. The inhabitants of Earth will realize there is a living God and He is a deadly, formidable force. The ensuing panic will confirm this. To those people who have set their face and lives <u>against</u> God's laws, this will come as a complete surprise – like a sneak attack. God is about to send panic through the camp of His enemies. Eventually, the wicked will be destroyed and the saints of God will at last, have peace on Earth! The occupation of *His* land will be over and the saints will live happily ever after.

4. The trumpets and the lamps

In ancient times, wars were not typically fought in darkness. It was too risky. Warfare was often hand-to-hand and close proximity to the enemy was necessary. In total darkness, it is impossible to tell a friend from an enemy! When Gideon's army startled the sleeping Midianites with shouting, 300 blazing lamps and 300 blaring trumpets, the Midianites instinctively knew they could not survive the battle. The Lord filled the hearts of Israel's enemy with overwhelming panic so that they fled in fear. This scenario also describes how the wicked will feel when the Great Tribulation begins. Fear will be everywhere. Anxiety will be out of control. Jesus said there will be distress that has no equal since the beginning of the world! (Matthew 24:21) Paul wrote, **"If we deliberately keep on sinning after we have received the knowledge of the truth, no sacrifice for sins is left, but only a fearful expectation of judgment and of raging fire that will consume the enemies of God."** (Hebrews 10:26,27) During the Great Tribulation, wicked people will have no rest, day or night (Revelation 14:11) because the Lord will fill their hearts with fear and anxiety.

During the Great Tribulation, God will send His servants, the 144,000, to proclaim the gospel of Jesus Christ to every kindred, tongue and nation. People who love the light illuminating the truth will step forward into the light and unite themselves with God's servants. The saints will have peace in the middle of the raging, chaotic storm. People who love iniquity will run for the cover of darkness so their deeds will not be seen in the light. In the darkness of sin, Paul writes there is a fearful expectation of judgment and raging fire. God will ensure it for He wants everyone to come to repentance. **"The Lord is not slow in keeping his promise, as some understand slowness. He is patient with you, not wanting anyone to perish, but everyone to come to repentance. But the day of the Lord will come like a thief. The heavens will disappear with a roar; the elements will be destroyed by fire, and the earth and everything in it will be laid bare. Since everything will be destroyed in this way, what kind of people ought you to be? You ought to live holy and godly lives."** (2 Peter 3:9-11)

The Cycles Continue

"Thus Midian was subdued before the Israelites and did not raise its head again. During Gideon's lifetime, the land enjoyed peace forty years. Jerub-Baal [Gideon] son of Joash went back home to live. He had seventy sons of his own, for he had many wives. His concubine, who lived in Shechem, also bore him a son, whom he named

Abimelech. Gideon son of Joash died at a good old age
and was buried in the tomb of his father Joash in
Ophrah of the Abiezrites. No sooner had Gideon died
than the Israelites again prostituted themselves to the
Baals. They set up Baal-Berith as their god and did not
remember the Lord their God, who had rescued them
from the hands of all their enemies on every side."
(Judges 8:28-34, insertion mine)   As far as I know, Gideon
holds the world record for having the largest number of children. (I do not know what happened – he *was* a timid guy at
first!) If Gideon had 70 sons (and 70 daughters), his offspring
would number around 140 children! In a way, Gideon's heri-
tage parallels the ministry of the 144,000. Through the efforts
of the 144,000, Abraham's seed will grow into a numberless
multitude during the Great Tribulation! ". . .And there before me was a great multitude that no one could count,
from every nation, tribe, people and language, standing
before the throne and in front of the Lamb. They were
wearing white robes and were holding palm branches in
their hands . . . . Then one of the elders asked me, 'These
in white robes – who are they, and where did they come
from?' I answered, 'Sir, you know.' And he said, 'These
are they who have come out of the great tribulation;
they have washed their robes and made them white in
the blood of the Lamb.' "   (Revelation 7:9, 13,14)

Regrettably, this story ends where it began. When Gideon
died, the *next* generation prostituted themselves to the Baals
again. If Israel's history proves anything, it proves how
quickly and how easily so many people can turn away from
obeying the Lord. We would do well to take note of this fact as
we draw near to the Great Day of the Lord! Remember, if we
had been there after Gideon died, some of us may have followed the rebellious majority.

Chapter 5

Elisha the Tishbite

"Elijah was a man just like us. He prayed earnestly that it would not rain, and it did not rain on the land for three and a half years. Again he prayed, and the heavens gave rain, and the earth produced its crops." (James 5:17,18)

The Old Testament prophet, Elijah, is mentioned 28 times in the New Testament. He had a popular legacy during the time of the apostles for at least six reasons: First, he was an ordinary man through whom God accomplished extraordinary things. As a young man, Elijah embarrassed the petulant King Ahab, angered his wicked wife, Jezebel, rebuked a nation almost totally given over to idolatry, and proved that Baal was no god. Second, they regarded Elijah to be a man of valor because he slaughtered 450 prophets of Baal after he proved they were false prophets. Third, Elijah was the first prophet in Old Testament times to raise a person from the dead. Fourth, God took Elijah to Heaven in a chariot of fire without experiencing death. Fifth, Peter, James and John saw Elijah on the mountain where Jesus was transfigured. Sixth, the last two verses of the book of Malachi end with the promise of a coming Elijah: **"See, I will send you the prophet Elijah before that great and dreadful day of the Lord comes. He will turn the hearts of the fathers to their children, and the hearts of the children to their fathers; or else I will come and strike the land with a curse."** (Malachi 4:5,6)

Elijah's ministry lasted a mere 24 years, but he is considered to be one of the greatest prophets in Old Testament times. His greatness had nothing to do with his family tree, his education, his personal wealth, or assets. In fact, James emphasizes this point by saying, **"Elijah was a man just like us."** Let there be no mistake – Elijah's greatness stemmed from God's greatness.

This is because he dedicated his life in service to God and glorified His holy name, especially at a time when such behavior was politically and religiously incorrect! Pay attention because Elijah's life story contains certain experiences that have powerful end time parallels.

How It Started

The twelve tribes of Israel were divided into two nations after Solomon died (around 920 B.C.). The popular and talented Jeroboam became king over ten tribes in the North, and Rehoboam, an insolent son of Solomon, was king over two tribes in the South. Both kings were evil minded in God's eyes and Jeroboam was considered more evil than Rehoboam. Jeroboam led Israel to commit great sins against God, the very One who had appointed him to be king over the ten tribes! (1 Kings 11:31) Jeroboam did not trust God's leadership. His goals were self-serving and he did not want the kingdom united. Jeroboam reasoned that Israel would not remain divided as long as the twelve tribes shared the same religion, so he resorted to a scheme to prevent Rehoboam from reuniting the twelve tribes. All Jews were required by law to go up to Jerusalem three times a year to observe Passover, Pentecost and the Feast of Tabernacles. Jeroboam knew that as long as his people regarded the high priest in Jerusalem (who favored the rule of Rehoboam) as their spiritual authority, his control over the ten tribes would not be secure. So, Jeroboam's scheme included displacing the religion of Israel with a "new" religion. Consider these words from the Bible:

"Jeroboam thought to himself, 'The kingdom will now likely revert to the house of David. If these people go up to offer sacrifices at the temple of the Lord in Jerusalem, they will again give their allegiance to their lord, Rehoboam king of Judah. They will kill me and return to king Rehoboam.' After seeking advice, the king made two golden calves. He said to the people, 'It is too much for you to go up to Jerusalem. Here are your gods, O Israel, who brought you up out of Egypt.' One he set up in Bethel, and the other in Dan. And this thing became a

sin; the people went even as far as Dan to worship the one there. **Jeroboam built shrines on high places and appointed priests from all sorts of people, even though they were not Levites.** He instituted a festival on the fifteenth day of the eighth month, like the festival held in Judah, and offered sacrifices on the altar. This he did in Bethel, sacrificing to the calves he had made. And at Bethel he also installed priests at the high places he had made. On the fifteenth day of the eighth month, a month of his own choosing, he offered sacrifices on the altar he had built at Bethel. So he instituted the festival for the Israelites and went up to the altar to make offerings." (1 Kings 12:26-33) Amazingly, the people accepted Jeroboam's new religion quickly. It is hard to believe that the Israelites accepted the new changes so readily, but they did. Their behavior demonstrates a profound truth about humankind. People can be led astray very quickly if their religious experience is not based on a personal understanding of God's Word. At the Great Tribulation, the "Jeroboam phenomenon" will occur again when the Antichrist forces everyone to participate in a new one-world religion.

From Bad to Worse

Jeroboam's blasphemy deeply offended God. One day, the old prophet, Ahijah, had a message for Jeroboam and he told Jeroboam's wife, **"Go, tell Jeroboam that this is what the Lord, the God of Israel, says: 'I raised you up from among the people and made you a leader over my people Israel. I tore the kingdom away from the house of David and gave it to you, but you have not been like my servant David, who kept my commands and followed me with all his heart, doing only what was right in my eyes. You have done more evil than all who lived before you. You have made for yourself other gods, idols made of metal; you have provoked me to anger and thrust me behind your back. Because of this, I am going to bring disaster on the house of Jeroboam. I will cut off from Jeroboam every last male in Israel – slave or free. I will burn up the house of Jeroboam as one burns dung, until it is all**

gone.' " (1 Kings 14:7-10) History records that Jeroboam ruled over the ten tribes for about 20 years before he was killed and his whole family slaughtered. After Jererboam's reign, a series of evil kings followed who were even more wicked than he was! Like a roller coaster gaining speed as it rolls down an incline, sin and apostasy continued to accelerate in Israel after Jeroboam died. About 35 years after Jeroboam was killed, a selfish and temperamental man named Ahab became king of Israel. His wife was a Sidonian woman, named Jezebel, who was notorious for her glamor and her ambition. The Bible says, **"There was never a man like Ahab, who sold himself to do evil in the eyes of the Lord, urged on by Jezebel his wife. He behaved in the vilest manner by going after idols, like the Amorites the Lord drove out before Israel."** (1 Kings 21:25,26) This background information on Israel's descent into decadence is important if we are to appreciate the appearing, loyalty, courage and actions of a young man, Elijah the Tishbite, who seemed to come out of nowhere.

Elijah Called

About 870 B.C., northern Israel's decadence had become so evil that God stepped in. He called a "country boy" from the remote desert territory of Gilead to be His spokesman. (God often chooses the most unlikely people to do awesome work.) As a youth, Elijah did not fill his mind with the foolishness of idolatry nor did he chase after the meaningless pleasures of carnal dissipation – pleasures which idolatry not only approved, but exalted. Elijah was devoted to God; deeply concerned and grieved by the idolatrous behavior of his people. Elijah knew that God's wrath toward Israel's behavior was long overdue. Elijah wanted to make a difference, but he recognized that he was just a youth and powerless to do anything about it. He had no influence, no pulpit and no money. To him, it seemed as if there was nothing he could do – except pray.

Elijah was a good student of God's Word and was intimately acquainted with the writings of Moses. He knew the covenant which the Lord gave to Moses at Mt. Sinai was conditional. At Sinai God said, **"If after all this you will not listen to me, I** will punish you for your sins seven times over. I will break down your stubborn pride and make the sky above you like iron and the ground beneath you like bronze. Your strength will be spent in vain, because your soil will not yield its crops, nor will the trees of the land yield their fruit." (Leviticus 26:18-20) Elijah was also acquainted with Solomon's published prayer which was proclaimed in Jerusalem when the temple was dedicated about 75 years earlier. Solomon had prayed, **"When the heavens are shut up and there is no rain because your people have sinned against you, and when they pray toward this place and confess your name and turn from their sin because you have afflicted them, then hear from heaven and forgive the sin of your servants, your people Israel. Teach them the right way to live, and send rain on the land you gave your people for an inheritance."** (1 Kings 8:35-36)

These and other Old Testament references gave Elijah an idea of how to pray for Israel. James writes, **"Elijah was a man just like us. He prayed earnestly that it would not rain, and it did not rain on the land for three and a half years."** (James 5:17) God was touched by the sincere prayer of Elijah. God was very aware of Israel's great wickedness, and in Elijah, God saw a sincere young man who was jealous for His honor. One day, God appeared before Elijah and told him that He had heard Elijah's prayers. Consequently, there would be no more rain until *Elijah* asked for it again. In other words, God gave Elijah the authority to determine when the famine would end! Wow! God placed enormous power in the hands of the young man from Tishbe. God told Elijah to go before Israel's king and deliver the message that the young prophet could control the rain. Think about this for a minute. This is like driving to Washington D.C., presuming that you would get access to the President of the United States, to tell him that it was not going to rain until you said so.

Elijah's faith was so compelling that it allowed him to take God at His word. Without hesitation, Elijah set out for Samaria to find King Ahab. Upon finding the king, Elijah approached him without introduction or savvy court etiquette and made this declaration: **"As the Lord, the God of Israel, lives, whom I serve, there will be neither dew nor rain in the next few years except at my word. . . ."** (1 Kings 17:1) That said, Elijah abruptly turned and departed. The king was surprised, then bemused. No doubt some of the king's attendants laughed out loud at the youthful folly of Elijah. "So here's a young man who thinks he can control the rain! Yeah, right!" Laughing and mocking, they joked, "That kid must have been out in the desert sun too long."

The Bible does not mention how long it took for the reality of the situation to dawn on Ahab. Depending on the season, 30 days without rain is not unusual in Palestine. Sixty days without rain is not deadly, but serious. Ninety days without rain and water shortages become a problem. It only takes about four months for serious signs of famine to appear. When it became evident that a famine was under way, the Holy Spirit brought a memory to the king and his officials of the sudden appearance and bold declaration of the young man. He seemed to come out of nowhere and disappeared just as fast. Where did this Elijah go? How could *he* control the rain? At first his claim appeared to be absolute folly, for no man could control the rain – or could they? As days continued to pass without a drop of rain, it became apparent that *someone* had caused the rain to cease!

End Time Parallel

There is an important end time parallel here. Revelation predicts that during the Great Tribulation, there will be no rain for three and a half years (the same length of time as in Elijah's day)! A worldwide famine is coming for the same reasons that a nationwide famine occurred in Elijah's day. Consider this text: **"These have power to shut heaven, that it rain not in the days of their prophecy: and have power over waters to turn them to blood, and to smite the earth with all plagues, as often as they will."** (Revelation 11:6, KJV)

Many Christians believe the Two Witnesses mentioned in Revelation are Moses and Elijah. My study has led me to a different conclusion. During the Great Tribulation, the Two Witnesses will empower 144,000 prophets of God to do miraculous things *just like* Moses and Elijah. Like Moses and Elijah, God's servants will exercise awesome supernatural powers *as they see fit.* Why will God grant so much power to His prophets during the Great Tribulation? I find there are two reasons: First, when incredible miracles can be performed at will, the miracle working person automatically gets a great deal of respect and attention. Second, when a miracle working person has something to say that is hard to accept, the miracles give added credibility. During the Great Tribulation, God will grant 144,000 prophets miracle working powers so that their antagonistic message will be carefully and thoughtfully considered by people whose minds are dull and darkened by idolatry and sin. Notice how God used this identical process during the days of Paul and Barnabas, **"So Paul and Barnabas spent considerable time there** [among the pagans in Iconium]**, speaking boldly for the Lord,** *who confirmed the message of his grace* **by enabling them to do miraculous signs and wonders."** (Acts 14:3, insertion mine, italics mine) Why did God give Paul and Barnabas miracle working powers? God gave these powers to Paul and Barnabas in Iconium to confirm the veracity of His messengers among the pagans.

"You Troubler of Israel"

During the third year of famine, Elijah could see that the famine was causing suffering which was overwhelming the whole land. Illness, malnutrition and death had decimated humanity and beasts. All the vegetation was either dead or dormant. Famine had swallowed up the land that once flowed with milk and honey. Elijah's heart was moved by the suffering of thousands of children. Starvation is a slow death and the untimely death of multitudes of sick people who wasted away with protracted suffering stirred Elijah's compassion. The fact that he had asked for the famine that caused all this suffering and carnage troubled Elijah's conscience! Incredibly, in spite of the famine and the suffering it caused, Israel still did not repent. When *he* could tolerate the decimation of his people no longer, Elijah petitioned the Lord to send rain. James writes, **"Again he** [Elijah] **prayed, and the heavens gave rain, and the earth produced its crops."** (James 5:18, insertion mine) This is a touching point. Every now and then, God allows a human being to experience His dilemma. God knows all about pain. When God called Abraham to offer his cherished son, Isaac, on an altar, God wanted Abraham to feel His own loss when He sacrificed His own dearly beloved Son on the cross. When God granted Elijah the power to control the famine in Israel, He also allowed Elijah to feel what He feels when He is left with no other remedy than to cause extreme suffering in getting humanity's attention. When Elijah had enough, he prayed for rain with the same intensity that he had prayed for famine.

The Bible says, **"After a long time, in the third year, the word of the Lord came to Elijah: 'Go and present yourself to Ahab, and I will send rain on the land.' So Elijah went to present himself to Ahab. . . ."** (1 Kings 18:1,2) As the famine continued, Elijah had become the most wanted man in Israel, dead or alive. In today's terms, Ahab and his cohorts regarded Elijah as a terrorist. To their way of thinking, Elijah had brought great harm to Israel. Tens of thousands of people were dead and the survivors were quick to blame Elijah! Ahab wanted Elijah captured and ordered that he be put to death at any cost. When Ahab learned that Elijah wanted to see him, he was surprised! The king went immediately so that he could capture the prophet. **"When he saw Elijah, he said to him, 'Is that you, you troubler of Israel?' 'I have not made trouble for Israel,' Elijah replied. 'But you and your father's family have. You have abandoned the Lord's commands and have followed the Baals.' "** (1 Kings 18:17,18) As the king approached Elijah, Ahab spoke first, blaming him for Israel's misery. Elijah did not blink, neither did he patronize the king. He simply confronted the king with unvarnished truth. At that moment, the king knew better than to lay hands on Elijah – he could sense that divine power rested upon the young man. More than three years of suffering kept the temperamental king from doing anything rash. Ahab had enough sense to realize that he was talking to a prophet of the Most High God who had control over the rain.

Think about this story for a minute. Who brought trouble upon Israel? Was it Ahab, Elijah or God? Ahab was exceedingly wicked, Elijah was vexed at Israel's apostasy, and God was angry with the degeneracy of the whole nation. In a sense, all three brought trouble upon Israel! God wanted repentance and reformation, Elijah wanted the God of Abraham to be exalted, and Ahab wanted relief. The point is that God honored Elijah's prayer *because* Israel violated His covenant! This famine did not occur simply because Elijah asked for it, nor was it just an arbitrary act of God. This famine did not occur because God loved Elijah and hated Israel. God does not work that way. Punishment by famine was a clearly stated provision contained in the covenant given at Mt. Sinai. When God honored Elijah's prayer, God was lawful and timely in doing so. Remember, this issue is also significant during the Great Tribulation. Famine is coming and the famine will be "just" because God is lawful in everything He does!

End Time Parallel

During the Great Tribulation, authorities will regard the 144,000 servants of God as "troublers of the nations." The 144,000 will be found throughout the world, each in his or her own land and tongue. (Presently, the approximate ratio is one of God's servants per 50,000 people.) As servants of God, they will be hated and hunted for the same reasons Elijah was hated and hunted: First, when God's servants exercise their miracle working powers, death and destruction will often follow. Remember the plagues that Moses called down on Egypt? Remember when Jesus exorcized the demons out of the two men in Matthew 8? (The demons were sent into a herd of pigs, which ran over a cliff and drowned themselves. Therefore, the owners of the pigs blamed Jesus for the great financial loss they suffered.) Remember when Paul and Silas set a young slave girl free from demonic possession and her owners became furious? (Acts 16) In a similar way, the 144,000 will use their miracle working powers as they see fit to overthrow demonic control. They will demolish foolish arguments and break the strongholds of demons with God's power! The 144,000 will anger people who love evil and people who are exposed by the 144,000 will hate them. People who try to lie to God, will be struck down by the Holy Spirit, just like Ananias and Sapphira. (Acts 5) God's servants will have awesome powers during their 1,260 days of empowerment. Please do not forget that God's servants will also perform miracles of healing and restoration. God's servants will receive a lot of respect from those who love truth, but they will be hated by people who love evil. Jesus said, **"Everyone who does evil hates the light, and will not come into the light for fear that his deeds will be exposed. But whoever lives by the truth comes into the light, so that it may be seen plainly that what he has done has been done through God."** (John 3:20,21)

The second reason the 144,000 will be regarded as "troublers of the nations" during the Great Tribulation centers around their antagonistic testimony. Because the Great Tribulation begins with several deadly judgments from God (global earthquake, meteoric firestorms, two asteroid impacts, etc.), religious and political leaders in every nation will use their authority of martial law to appease God. In other words, a time is coming when the religious and political leaders of the world will mandate the worship of God in hopes that He will be appeased and cease His horrific judgments. However, the 144,000 will proclaim God's truth with unvarnished clarity and their opposition to the laws of the land will anger authorities. Like Elijah, God's servants during the end time will be regarded as "troublers of the nations" and the authorities will hunt them down to be jailed or killed.

The Showdown

Back to Elijah's story: When King Ahab approached the young prophet, Elijah did not enter into a conversation with Ahab. There was nothing to discuss. Elijah spoke to the king as though he were a servant. He said, **" 'Now summon the people from all over Israel to meet me on Mount Carmel. And bring the four hundred and fifty prophets of Baal and the four hundred prophets of Asherah, who eat at Jezebel's table.' So Ahab sent word throughout all Israel**

and assembled the prophets on Mount Carmel." (1 Kings 18:19,20) When the hand of God rests upon a person, smart kings pay attention! In this case, the prophet gave the orders and the king obeyed.

When the appointed day came, thousands of people gathered on Mount Carmel for a showdown between Baal and Jehovah. Consider the scene: There stood the king with his 450 false prophets. Elijah, however, stood alone. For three and a half years the prophets of Baal and Asherah had been unable to produce rain! Now, on the mountain top, would Baal respond to the corporate invocation of his prophets to prove his superiority over Jehovah? From a human interest point of view, the contest must have been very interesting to watch. On one side stood 850 prophets holding up religious icons, smoking censers and wearing imposing priestly regalia. On the other side stood a country boy from Tishbe wearing the course garment of a poor man. **"Elijah went before the people and said, 'How long will you waver between two opinions? If the Lord is God, follow him; but if Baal is God, follow him.' But the people said nothing. Then Elijah said to them, 'I am the only one of the Lord's prophets left, but Baal has four hundred and fifty prophets. Get two bulls for us. Let them choose one for themselves, and let them cut it into pieces and put it on the wood but not set fire to it. I will prepare the other bull and put it on the wood but not set fire to it. Then you call on the name of your god, and I will call on the name of the Lord. The god who answers by fire – he is God.' Then all the people said, 'What you say is good.' Elijah said to the prophets of Baal, 'Choose one of the bulls and prepare it first, since there are so many of you. Call on the name of your god, but do not** [deceitfully] **light the fire.' "** (1 Kings 18:21-25, insertion mine)

The prophets of Baal could not weasel out of Elijah's offer or the people would have understood the deception and stoned them. **"So they** [the prophets of Baal] **took the bull given them and prepared it. Then they called on the name of Baal from morning till noon. 'O Baal, answer us!' they shouted.**

But there was no response; no one answered. And they
danced around the altar they had made. At noon Elijah
began to taunt them. 'Shout louder!' he said. 'Surely he is
a god! Perhaps he is deep in thought, or busy, or traveling. Maybe he is sleeping and must be awakened.' So they
shouted louder and slashed themselves with swords and
spears, as was their custom, until their blood flowed.
Midday passed, and they continued their frantic proph-
esying until the time for the evening sacrifice. But there
was no response, no one answered, no one paid attention." (1 Kings 18:26-30, insertion mine) Can you imagine how
disgusted the people must have been after watching their 450
prophets spend the whole day dancing and shouting – and after
it was all said and done, there was not even a spark!

Have you ever seen a person forced into the admission that his
religion was false? False religion is vanity, a figment of fallen
imagination. Carnal man needs God, but he prefers a god that
condones carnal behavior! False religion appeals to the carnal
nature because it offers loopholes to justify sin and wrong doing.
The carnal heart is inherently opposed to God's commandments.
(Romans 8) The carnal mind thinks nothing of blaspheming
God and usurping His authority. The carnal heart does not
hesitate to trash God's wisdom by presumptuously thinking it
knows more than God and how things ought to be done. False
religion accommodates the carnal heart, making it always
popular with the masses. When Jeroboam installed a foreign
religion within Israel, the nation went along with the religion
because the majority of the nation's population was carnal in
nature. When Elijah put the priests of Baal to the test on
Mount Carmel, he knew a showdown would not change the
hearts of the vast majority of the people. However, he hoped
that by proving Baal to be a false god, some people might repent
and humbly submit to God's authority.

Elijah's Turn

"Then Elijah said to all the people, 'Come here to me.' They
came to him, and he repaired the altar of the Lord, which
was in ruins. Elijah took twelve stones, one for each of the

tribes descended from Jacob, to whom the word of the
Lord had come, saying, 'Your name shall be Israel.' With the
stones he built an altar in the name of the Lord, and he dug
a trench around it large enough to hold two seahs [about
3.25 gallons] of seed. He arranged the wood, cut the bull into
pieces and laid it on the wood. Then he said to them, 'Fill
four large jars with water and pour it on the offering and
on the wood.' 'Do it again,' he said, and they did it again.
'Do it a third time,' he ordered, and they did it the third
time. The water ran down around the altar and even filled
the trench. At the time of [the evening] sacrifice, the prophet
Elijah stepped forward and prayed: 'O Lord, God of
Abraham, Isaac and Israel, let it be known today that you
are God in Israel and that I am your servant and have done
all these things at your command. Answer me, O Lord,
answer me, so these people will know that you, O Lord, are
God, and that you are turning their hearts back again.'
Then the fire of the Lord fell and burned up the sacrifice,
the wood, the stones and the soil, and also licked up the
water in the trench. When all the people saw this, they fell
prostrate and cried, 'The Lord [Jehovah]—he is God! The
Lord [Jehovah]—he is God!' " (1 Kings 18:30-39, insertions
mine)

Elijah was a man of faith. He not only depended on the Lord's
response to his prayer, but his faith also anticipated God's
response. The bolt of fire that fell from Heaven proved Baal was
a false god in a split second. No words were needed. Even Ahab
was speechless. What else could the people say except that "The
Lord – He is God." **"Then Elijah commanded them, 'Seize
the prophets of Baal. Don't let anyone get away!' They
seized them, and Elijah had them brought down to the
Kishon Valley and slaughtered there."** (1 Kings 18:40) The
only way to eliminate the influence of false religion is to destroy
its preachers. (Of course, the same will be said of God's servants during the Great Tribulation. See John 16.) When the
people affirmed that Jehovah was God, Elijah lawfully ordered
the execution of the prophets of Baal on the basis of God's
authority in Deuteronomy 13. **"If a prophet, or one who**

foretells by dreams, appears among you and announces to you a miraculous sign or wonder, and if the sign or wonder of which he has spoken takes place, and he says, 'Let us follow other gods' (gods you have not known) 'and let us worship them,' you must not listen to the words of that prophet or dreamer. The Lord your God is testing you to find out whether you love him with all your heart and with all your soul. It is the Lord your God you must follow, and him you must revere. Keep his commands and obey him; serve him and hold fast to him. That prophet or dreamer must be put to death, because he preached rebellion against the Lord your God, who brought you out of Egypt and redeemed you from the land of slavery; he has tried to turn you from the way the Lord your God commanded you to follow. You must purge the evil from among you." (Deuteronomy 13:1-5)

Critical End Time Parallel

The fire-from-Heaven display in Elijah's day has a critical end time parallel. In fact, the primary reason for this study on Elijah centers on this fire-from-Heaven parallel. Here is the problem: A time is coming when the devil [the Antichrist] will be allowed to appear on Earth. He will masquerade as God and to prove his assumed divinity, the devil will do many miracles, signs and wonders. His crowning deception will be his ability to call fire down from Heaven in full view of men! Notice this text: **"And he** [the lamb-like beast] **performed great and miraculous signs,** *even causing fire to come down from heaven to earth in full view of men.* **Because of the signs he was given power to do on behalf of the first beast, he deceived the inhabitants of the earth** [into thinking he was Almighty God.] **He ordered them to set up an image in honor of the beast who was wounded by the sword and yet lived."** (Revelation 13:13,14, insertions and italics mine) Why is fire-from-Heaven a problem? The problem is that God's servants *will not* be able to respond to this deception! This miracle will trump any miracle which God's servants will be allowed to do. This is God's plan and here is an explanation:

During the Great Tribulation, there will be "a showdown of gods." According to Bible prophecy, the setting for this show-down unfolds like this: A series of devastating judgments from God will cause the Great Tribulation. About 1.5 billion people will be killed by the initial wave of these judgments. At that time, God's 144,000 servants will be empowered to proclaim the gospel (the terms and conditions of salvation). The 144,000 will testify of the coming kingdom of Christ. The religious and political leaders of each nation will form a crisis government and in an attempt to appease the wrath of Almighty God, they will impose a series of laws upon the inhabitants within each respective nation. These laws will require people to honor and worship God. During this time, the 144,000 will also command the human race to worship God, but the worship required by the laws of men will be contrary to the law of God. This is the setting – a great controversy over worship during the Great Tribulation.

The gospel of Jesus Christ will put the 144,000 servants of God and their followers in a position that will be at odds with the religions and governments of the world. People who accept the gospel presented by the 144,000 will be punished and perse-cuted for rebelling against the laws of the land. During the first 30 months of the Great Tribulation, the gospel will go power-fully throughout the world. Most of the world will hear and make a decision about the everlasting gospel. After most of the people have rejected the gospel, the showdown of gods then occurs. It happens this way: God permits the devil [the Anti-christ] and his angels to *physically* appear on Earth. Remem-ber, a majority of the world **will have heard and already rejected** the truth about the worship which God requires. Study the words of Paul: **"They** [the majority] **perish because they refused to love the truth and so be saved. For this reason God sends them a powerful delusion so that they will believe the lie and so that all will be condemned who have not believed the truth but have delighted in wick-edness."** (2 Thessalonians 2:10-12, insertion mine) This verse indicates two things: First, the people of Earth "refused to love the truth." Obviously, you cannot refuse something you have not heard or do not understand. So, Paul is talking about willful defiance. Second, because people have defiantly rejected truth, God sends a powerful delusion! Why does God send a powerful delusion to the wicked?

God allows the devil to physically appear before the people of Earth because God wants the world to see who they are actually worshiping if they refuse to worship God. God uses the devil, who masquerades as God, to separate His sheep from the goats. People who love truth and righteousness will worship God. Those who defy God will be deceived by the fire-from-Heaven miracle, thinking the devil is God! **"Because of the signs he was given power to do on behalf of the first beast, he deceived the inhabitants of the Earth...."** (Revelation 13:14)

An Angel of Light

When Satan appears on Earth claiming to be God, his radiant countenance will so dazzle the people of Earth that many will believe his claims that he is God based on his appearance alone. Paul says, **"... for Satan himself masquerades as an angel of light."** (2 Corinthians 11:14) Revelation states that when Satan appears, he will be so dazzling that most people will be awestruck when they actually see him! John writes, **"... The inhabitants of the Earth whose names have not been written in the book of life from the creation of the world will be *astonished* when they see the beast...."** (Revelation 17:8, italics mine.)

Satan Works Miracles, Signs and Wonders

Satan's first work after appearing "in the flesh" as a magnificent God-man will be to convince the world that he is divine – that he is actually God. Paul warns, **"Don't let anyone deceive you in any way, for that day (the second coming) will not come until the rebellion occurs and the man of lawlessness is revealed, the man doomed to destruction. He opposes and exalts himself over everything that is called God or is worshiped, and even sets himself up in God's temple, proclaiming himself to be God .... The** coming of the lawless one will be in accordance with the work of Satan displayed in all kinds of counterfeit miracles, signs and wonders, and in every sort of evil that deceives those who are perishing. They perish because they refused to love the truth and so be saved." (2 Thessalonians 2:3,4,9,10)

Calls Fire Down out of Heaven

The one miracle that Satan will use above all others to convince the wicked that he is God will be to call fire down out of Heaven at will! Because God does not allow His 144,000 servants to call fire down from Heaven, the devil's use of this miracle will make his deception secure for billions of people. John says, **"And he performed great and miraculous signs, even causing fire to come down from heaven to Earth in full view of men. Because of the signs he was given power to do on behalf of the first beast, he deceived the inhabitants of the Earth . . . ."** (Revelation 13:13,14) Satan will make every effort to deceive the world into believing that he alone is worthy of worship. This is why God grants the devil the power to call fire down from Heaven. If I summarize what God might say, perhaps He would express the problem this way: If men and women refuse to love and obey the clearest evidences of truth and if they refuse to honor Me as their Creator and Redeemer, then I will grant them their evil and rebellious desires. I will send them the "father of rebellion." Let them chase after their miracles instead of truth. Since humanity loves lies more than truth, I will grant Lucifer, the father of lies, the power to perform the ultimate miracle. The wicked will see fire fall from Heaven upon command and they will receive this miracle as "proof of divinity." By doing this, the wicked will worship and receive Satan as their god of choice and seal their eternal fate.

Then the Rain Came

In Elijah's day, the famine proved that Baal could not send water from Heaven. The all-day service on Mount Carmel also proved that Baal could not send fire from Heaven. The verdict was clear, Baal was no god. Baal was merely a figment of foolish imagination. No doubt, some of the older people remembered the words of the covenant that had been spoken at Mt. Sinai. The Lord said, **"If you follow my decrees and are careful to obey my commands, I will send you rain in its season, and the ground will yield its crops and the trees of the field their fruit. Your threshing will continue until grape harvest and the grape harvest will continue until planting, and you will eat all the food you want and live in safety in your land."** (Leviticus 26:3-5) Everyone knew that day that Israel's apostasy and Israel's famine were inseparably linked. In the last days, people who love truth will understand this linkage during the Great Tribulation.

After the evening service was completed, **"Elijah said to Ahab, 'Go, eat and drink, for there is the sound of a heavy rain.' So Ahab went off to eat and drink, but Elijah climbed to the top of Carmel, bent down to the ground and put his face between his knees. 'Go and look toward the sea,' he told his servant. And he went up and looked. 'There is nothing there,' he said. Seven times Elijah said, 'Go back.' The seventh time the servant reported, 'A cloud as small as a man's hand is rising from the sea.' So Elijah said, 'Go and tell Ahab, "Hitch up your chariot and go down before the rain stops you."' Meanwhile, the sky grew black with clouds, the wind rose, a heavy rain came on and Ahab rode off to Jezreel. The power of the Lord came upon Elijah and, tucking his cloak into his belt, he ran ahead of Ahab all the way** [about 20 miles] **to Jezreel."** (1 Kings 18:41-46, insertion mine) Ahab and his entourage must have been astonished to see Elijah outrun their horses all the way to Jezreel! What man can outrun horses for 20 miles?

When Elijah climbed to the top of the mountain to ask for rain, the Lord did not respond to His servant immediately. God tested the faith and endurance of Elijah just like He tested the faith and endurance of Moses when Moses struck the rock. Elijah's faith did not wane. He kept pressing his petition to the Lord to send rain. There is an important parallel for all of us in this story. It is our privilege to press our heartfelt petitions before the Lord and there is good news! God responds. I believe there is a lot of confusion about the purpose and privilege of prayer among Christians. Here are ten short statements to consider:

1. Prayer does not entice God to do things that are not in our best interest.

2. Prayer does not give God permission to do things. God is sovereign.

3. Prayer does not nullify the cause and effect laws that God created because of sin.

4. Prayer does not make God love us more.

5. God will not violate the will of another person because of intercessory prayer.

6. The highest motive for prayer is to be used by God, not to use God.

7. God responds in some way to *every* sincere prayer. Sometimes, it takes a while to figure out how He is responding or how He responded.

8. God closes His ears to our prayers if we defy the convictions of the Holy Spirit.

9. Frequent prayer changes us, not God. Prayer opens our hearts and minds to the greater and wiser will of God. Through prayer God gives us strength to better reflect His character of love when we are tested. Through prayer God gives us courage and peace to trust in His control over matters that are beyond our control. One of the hardest things to believe is that God is intimately involved when everything is going wrong in our life. Prayer can transform doubt into trust.

10. Sometimes, in response to a specific petition, God will dramatically alter the natural outcome of an event to make a statement. (We call these acts of God, "miracles.") But to remain fair to the millions of suffering people who pray for

miracles every day, God does not casually alter the rules which He ordained by violating the cause and effect rules. If the cause and effect rules were violated frequently in the universe, there would be unintelligible chaos everywhere! Think about this. If God frequently violated the cause and effect rules, miracles would not be recognized because no one would know if God had averted a natural consequence or not. Everything favorable would be a miracle and everything unfavorable would also be a miracle, so miracles would not have the amazing effect they have on people today.

I believe the Lord waited to send rain until Elijah prayed seven times in order to humble His servant. God had publicly exalted Elijah, as no other prophet, when He sent fire from Heaven at Elijah's request. Now, God humbled His prophet on the same day by making him beg for rain. The never-to-be-forgotten point here is that God is not our servant. He is forever God and we never rise higher, even on Mount Carmel, than the position of servant. Elijah was an ordinary man who became great because Elijah's God was great.

Epilog

"Now Ahab told Jezebel everything Elijah had done and how he had killed all the prophets with the sword. So Jezebel sent a messenger to Elijah to say, 'May the gods deal with me, be it ever so severely, if by this time tomorrow I do not make your life like that of one of them.' Elijah was afraid and ran for his life." (1 Kings 19:1-3)

This chapter has to close and I could not think of a better stopping place than Elijah running from Jezebel. After running faster than horses for the 20 miles to Jezreel, the prophet probably felt his best defense against Jezebel was running for his life. The contradiction within humankind, even in God's servants, is bravery and boldness for one problem versus weakness and anxiety. May God help us realize that unless we are filled with His presence and strength each day – our flesh is weak, very weak.

Chapter 6

Saul – Good Heart Wrong Head

This book has focused on Bible characters whose experiences have significant end time parallels, and the life of the apostle Paul is no exception. To summarize the life of Saul before his conversion into a single sound bite, I would say, "good heart, wrong head." If I were to sum up the life of Saul after conversion, I would say, "whole heart, right head." The story of Saul's transformation has dimensions that every Christian should consider because a complete paradigm shift is no small thing.

As a Child

Bible students know few facts about Saul's childhood. Most scholars believe that he was born about A.D. 12 in the coastal city of Tarsus. Tarsus was near the northeast corner of the Mediterranean Sea at a location about 250 miles southeast of where Ankara, Turkey is today. Saul belonged to the tribe of Benjamin, a tribe well known for its fierce and zealous devotion. (Genesis 49:27; Judges 20:15,16) Saul's parents may have named him after the first king of Israel, who was also a descendent from the tribe of Benjamin. Because Pompey made Tarsus the capital of the Roman province of Cilicia in 67 B.C., Saul came into this world having two identities: He was a Jew by nationality, and he was also a Roman citizen. This unique combination ultimately enabled Paul to travel and speak for God in places and languages that few people could have done at that time. As a city, Tarsus was noted for its advanced schools, including a respected school in Stoic philosophy. The pride of Tarsus was its academic prowess and this son of Tarsus was no embarrassment.

As a young man, Saul decided to serve God as a rabbi. His passion for learning was as great as his ability to absorb and comprehend. As a lad, Saul probably traveled to Jerusalem with his father for the appointed feasts. It must have been an awe inspiring treat for young Saul to see the grandeur of the temple and the fascinating services the priests conducted. Perhaps it was these events that inspired Saul to dedicate himself to God's service. Saul was not a Levite, so he could not become a priest, however, he could do the next best thing and become a member of the Pharisee party.

After completing studies in Tarsus, he was accepted into the school taught by the Pharisee scholars in Jerusalem. There, he studied under the famous teacher, Gamaliel. (Acts 22:3) I believe Saul was about 18 when he arrived in Jerusalem, shortly after Jesus had ascended to Heaven in A.D. 30. Saul was deeply passionate about his religion and being accustomed to a life of self denial, he paid careful attention to right doing. Saul was totally committed to becoming a Pharisee. He was a zealot in every detail; energetic, intense and ideological. He was an exemplary student, and because he was intellectually superior, his teachers were confident this young man would have a bright future within their ranks. It has been said that "love is blind." If this is so, then Saul's love for his religion led him to be totally convinced of the inerrancy of the Pharisaical doctrines and the righteousness of his ways. Years later he wrote, ". . . **If anyone else thinks he has reasons to put confidence in the flesh, I have more: circumcised on the eighth day, of the people of Israel, of the tribe of Benjamin, a Hebrew of Hebrews; in regard to the law, a Pharisee; as for zeal, persecuting the church; as for legalistic righteousness, faultless."** (Philippians 3:4-6)

Religious Parties

In Saul's day, Israel consisted of several religious sects (or denominations) much like Protestantism today. Tensions between various sects were openly hostile and militant toward each other at times. Constant friction made it difficult for Rome to govern Jerusalem. Because Jerusalem was a city of *relatives* having competing views about God, it was a contentious place in which to live. No doubt this caustic environment was one reason why John the Baptist conducted his meetings in the desert.

When Saul arrived in Jerusalem for advanced schooling, two religious parties dominated the scene. As you might expect, these two parties represented the liberals and the conservatives. The Pharisee party, to which Saul had pledged himself, was known for its pious commitment to righteousness through austerity and rigor. As conservatives, they were zealous for righteous living and were quick to condemn anyone who violated *their* rules of righteousness. (Mark 2) They believed righteousness was of utmost importance because they thought unrighteous people could not receive eternal life. Therefore, the Pharisees were constantly codifying righteousness by defining rules for every aspect of life. For example, when it came to Sabbath observance, the Pharisees had codified more than 400 rules for proper Sabbath observance. *The Pharisees were convinced that life in the hereafter was only possible through rigorous obedience to God's laws.* Their winning argument was: "Would God grant eternal life to a sinner who chose to live in ignorance and defiance to His laws?" Because Israel had a long history of apostasy, the Pharisees "reasoned" that using a heavy legalistic doctrine would "help" the Jews prevent apostasy from occurring again. (Matthew 23) *It is ironic that the greatest fear of the Pharisees was apostasy.*

The religion of the Pharisees required conformity to rules rather than purity of heart. (Matthew 3:7-10) To them, a zeal for conformity was the evidence of a "new heart" mentioned by Ezekiel. (Ezekiel 18:31; Jeremiah 31:33) The Pharisees loved religion; it was their God. They believed that if a "righteous person" happened to have any "unknown" sin in his life, the righteousness of Abraham, their father, covered any deficit. (Genesis 15:6; Luke 3:8) Perhaps Saul was attracted to the Pharisees because like himself, they were dogmatic and their thirst for advanced education was insatiable. (John 5:39,40; 2 Timothy 3:7) The Pharisees considered the Old Testament, plus the writings and traditions of the rabbis to be the "Word of God." Therefore, the Pharisees staunchly defended the traditions and orthodoxy of Judaism more aggressively than any other party in Israel.

The other leading party of the time, the Sadducees, was also legalistic and politically powerful, but in a different way than the Pharisees. The Sadducees did not believe in a hereafter. Consequently, they were self-indulgent and focused on obtaining wealth, pleasure, status and comfort. Even more, they rejected all but the first five books of the Old Testament. The Sadducees were legalistic pragmatists. For example, they saw nothing wrong with hiring Gentiles to work for them on Sabbath, as long as none of the Gentiles lived within their gates. (Exodus 20:10) The Sadducees despised the austere lifestyle of the Pharisees and they constantly argued with them over theological differences. Overall, it seemed that the Sadducees held control of Israel politically, while the the Pharisees held control over the people religiously.

A.D. 30 Christianity Begins to Grow

Before we examine Saul's conversion on the road to Damascus, we need to highlight developments that happened in Jerusalem while Saul was attending school. After the apostles baptized 3,000 believers into the kingdom of God on that great day of Pentecost in A.D. 30, the Christian movement in Jerusalem began to expand rapidly. Over the next four years, various disciples of Jesus were publically humiliated and punished for promoting what was considered an inflammatory religion that was highly critical of Jewish leaders and the teachings of Judaism. As is so often the case, the more Jewish leaders persecuted the disciples of Jesus, the more popular they became!

The Bible says, **"The apostles performed many miraculous signs and wonders among the people. And all the believers used to meet together in Solomon's Colonnade** [in the temple complex]**."** (Acts 5:12, insertion mine) Proselytizing in the temple and healing the sick on the streets produced a large number of converts. As Christianity grew in popularity in Jerusalem, the Sadducees became highly agitated. Their political support was eroding. The Pharisees were also alarmed because people called them enemies of God. The Christian movement was different than anything Jewish leaders had ever seen before. The disciples of Jesus were performing *genuine* miracles daily, just like Jesus had done! People who had suffered from lifelong illness were being healed, right before the eyes of people who were intimately acquainted with their illness. These wonderful and joyous manifestations of divine power were the talk of the town and crowds flocked to hear and see what the disciples of Jesus were doing and saying.

". . . People brought the sick into the streets and laid them on beds and mats so that at least Peter's shadow might fall on some of them as he passed by. Crowds gathered also from the towns around Jerusalem, bringing their sick and those tormented by evil spirits, and all of them were healed." (Acts 5:15,16) Boldly, Peter and the disciples spoke and performed miracles and Jewish authorities could not rebuff them. Christians were teaching salvation through belief in Jesus Christ. They were preaching to the Jewish people that Jesus was man's High Priest and that temple rituals were no longer necessary. The Christians exclaimed that Pharisees and Sadducees had slain the Lamb of God! Over the course of time, the Pharisees and the Sadducees held several meetings to discuss proposals that would shut down the growth of Christianity. Christian doctrine and influence was threatening the survival of Judaism and something had to be done.

The Sanhedrin

The Sanhedrin was Israel's highest court. The 71 members of the Sanhedrin came from all religious parties according to election and/or bribery. The Romans granted the Jews (and other similar tribal nations) a limited amount of civil power to deal with their own people. As far as the Romans were concerned, tribal nations were allowed to impose their cultural laws as long as they stayed within the higher laws of Rome. Granting this type of authority freed the Romans from the onerous chore of passing judgment on meaningless and disputable matters like religion. However, there was one law above all others that Rome imposed on all tribal nations. The Romans made it clear that tribal nations did not have the power to punish *any* Roman citizen. Every Roman citizen had the right to appeal to Caesar.

You may recall that after Peter denied being a follower of Jesus in Pilate's judgment hall early Friday morning before the crucifixion, Peter's remorse and broken spirit allowed him to have a "born again" conversion that weekend. (John 21:15-19) The Lord restored Peter's credibility among the disciples by empowering him with enormous Holy Spirit power. Thus, it was Peter who boldly led the way at Pentecost when 3,000 souls were baptized. Later on, God used Peter again in a powerful way when the Holy Spirit revealed to him the deceptions of Ananias and Sapphira. Their sudden death had a profound impact on the early church. (Acts 5) For all his faults and weaknesses, Peter had certain qualities the Lord could use, but only *after* Peter was converted. Peter became bold in God's grace and strength, no longer depending on his own arms of flesh. Peter was a "black and white" kind of a guy, leaving no gray areas in his mind. He did not mince words about the atrocities of Jewish leaders, especially when telling the Jews about the murder of Jesus. Peter's boldness had a price for which he was arrested and imprisoned, but an angel miraculously freed him from the chains of his captors during the night. A few days later, Peter rallied the apostles and they went out on the streets of Jerusalem again. No human can thwart this kind of determination and power.

When the Sanhedrin heard that Peter was out of prison and that he and the apostles were healing the sick on the streets of Jerusalem *again*, they immediately sent a captain and soldiers for him. Notice what the Bible says, **"At that, the captain went with his officers and brought the apostles. They did not use force, because they feared that the people**

would stone them. **Having brought the apostles, they
made them appear before the Sanhedrin to be questioned by the high priest. 'We gave you strict orders not
to teach in this name,' he said. 'Yet you have filled
Jerusalem with your teaching and are determined to
make us guilty of this man's blood.' Peter and the other
apostles replied** [in never-to-be-forgotten words]: **'We must
obey God rather than men! The God of our fathers
raised Jesus from the dead – whom you had killed by
hanging him on a tree. God exalted him to his own right
hand as Prince and Savior that he might give repentance and forgiveness of sins to Israel. We are witnesses
of these things, and so is the Holy Spirit, whom God has
given to those who obey him.' When they heard this,
they** [members of the Sanhedrin] **were furious and wanted
to put them to death."** (Acts 5:26-33, insertions mine)

The Bible record continues: **"But a Pharisee named
Gamaliel, a teacher of the law, who was honored by all
the people, stood up in the Sanhedrin and ordered that
the men be put outside for a little while.   Then he ad-
dressed them: 'Men of Israel, consider carefully what
you intend to do to these men. Some time ago Theudas
appeared, claiming to be somebody, and about four
hundred men rallied to him. He was killed, all his followers were dispersed, and it all came to nothing. After
him, Judas the Galilean appeared in the days of the
census and led a band of people in revolt. He too was
killed, and all his followers were scattered. Therefore,
in the present case I advise you: Leave these men alone!
Let them go! For if their purpose or activity is of human
origin, it will fail. But if it is from God, you will not be
able to stop these men; you will only find yourselves
fighting against God.' "** (Acts 5:34-39)

The wisdom of Gamaliel is legendary for good reason. No
wonder Saul wanted to sit at his feet. The words and influence
of Gamaliel during this meeting brings up a very important
point. Consider this: For centuries, Christians have viewed

the Pharisees with a certain amount of contempt. This contempt rises from the New Testament. Christians believe that Jesus is "God in the flesh." They find the Pharisees and the Sadducees to be so blinded by their religious dogma that they cannot even see that Jesus is the Messiah. Consequently, a certain amount of contempt has been held down through the centuries for those who participated in Christ's death. But is this Christian contempt for the Jews appropriately placed? Consider this:

Confrontation

Jesus came to Earth at God's appointed time. His birth was not a random event. The timing of Jesus' birth and ministry on Earth was *predetermined* so that Jesus could challenge the finest religious system that *man* could produce. (Galatians 4:4) God wanted to demonstrate the reaction and behavior of the world's best religious system when confronted with truth. *In other words, the contest between Jesus and the Pharisees is a parallel of Jesus versus any religious system!* This is an end time parallel that everyone should consider. Some of the Pharisees, like Gamaliel, were sincere and devout. The Jewish people respected them because they were dedicated to selfless sacrifice for the service of God. The Pharisee party was horribly misguided, but Gamaliel was not an evil man. He was a spiritual man, a good man in a religious system that comingled the doctrines of men with the truth of God. (Mark 7:7) As a Pharisee, Gamaliel had a "good heart" but a "wrong head" when it came to understanding the fulfillment of Scripture. His comments prove that he wondered in his heart if Jesus might be the Messiah.

A Christian cannot appreciate the contest between Jesus and the Pharisees until he/she also discovers that he/she actually suffers from the same problems that afflicted the Pharisees. A blind man cannot see. A blind man cannot see what he should see unless, (a) there is someone to open his eyes, and (b) he is willing to open his eyes. When people are blinded by the certainty of their own religious dogma, they cannot see or understand their own blindness! This is a problem that every human being must wrestle with. The Pharisees were convinced they were right and everyone else was wrong. Jesus came into their world and spoke truth. The result was a deadly confrontation. Here is a profound thought: Our ability to understand truth is proportional to our willingness to consider truth. We cannot mature in an understanding of truth unless we are willing to submit to what we have learned. We cannot enjoy the freedom and joy of truth until we come to a place in life where we decide to follow truth – no matter what it is, or what it costs.

The Pharisee Test

There are some pharisaical ways in every human being. Here is a short test that demonstrates this. The Pharisees hated Jesus for three reasons: First, Jesus did not show reverence for the ideas they respected. Jesus insulted their piety, their culture, their ideas about salvation and their overall view of God. (If Jesus came into *your* church and did this to *you*, how would you react?) Second, Jesus embarrassed the Pharisees by condemning them with their own words. Jesus caused people to have less respect for the Pharisees with each episode of embarrassment. Jesus continually demonstrated how the religion of the Pharisees was driven by vanity. (If Jesus embarrassed your church leaders every time they made a religious statement, how would you feel?) Third, Jesus performed miracles every day to back up His outrageous claims. Since the Pharisees could not perform miracles, Jesus' actions further humiliated the Pharisees in the eyes of the people by proving they were spiritually devoid of God's power. (What would your church leaders do with a miracle working person in their midst who taught a strange and different doctrine?) To be confronted with God and His truth is not a casual experience. During the Great Tribulation, the confronting presence of truth will push every person into either defiant rebellion or complete submission. There will be no middle ground. Jesus told His disciples, **"For whoever is not against us is for us."** (Mark 9:40)

"The Way"

This bold, new Christian belief system threatened the culture
and traditional ways of the Jews, so the Pharisees and
Sadducees united against a common enemy called "The Way."
The Christian movement was initially called "The Way" be-
cause Jesus said, **". . . I am *the way* and the truth and the
life. No one comes to the Father except through me."**
(John 14:6, italics mine) As time passed, members of "The
Way" became known as "Christians." (Acts 11:26)

During the first four years of Christian growth in Jerusalem,
Saul was a graduate student in the school of the Pharisees. As
tensions mounted between Jews and Christians, young Saul, a
zealous ideologue, came to despise Christians because their
actions were tearing down the very institution to which he had
dedicated his life. By the end of A.D. 33, the Sanhedrin was
forced to ignore Gamaliel's words. The Sanhedrin finally
concluded that the death penalty must be administered to all
dissidents belonging to "The Way" or chaos would ultimately
bring the wrath of Rome down upon Jerusalem.

> **Note:** The Romans required tribal nations to keep peace in their
> cities. If a civil disturbance required the presence and services of
> the Roman army, the Romans would destroy the entire city.
> Total destruction was Rome's way. This action prevented many
> problems from reappearing in the future. Of course, loot from the
> city was then used to pay Rome's mercenary soldiers.

Dealing with Dissidence

Every group of people, whether it be religious or political, faces
dissidence at some point in time. If the group does not remove
defiant dissidents, division and dissipation will ultimately
occur. Because Christians chose to defy the demands of the
Sanhedrin, the Sanhedrin was forced to punish Christians.
They had no option but to destroy the apostles and their followers to protect their religion and their city! There is a powerful end time parallel here. During the Great Tribulation,
religious and political leaders will unite and attempt to destroy
the opposition created by God's servants.

Divine Authority

Deuteronomy 13 contains the directions God gave to Moses for
dealing with dissident behavior. The chapter is divided into
two parts. The first part concerns false prophets and the
second part concerns misguided leaders or laymen. The
Sanhedrin used Deuteronomy 13 to justify their execution of
Jesus and later, they justified their persecution of the apostles
with this same chapter. There is also an end time parallel
here. During the Great Tribulation, God will confront the
great religions of the world with His truth. These institutions
will not be able to accept His truth, without destroying what
they stand for, any more than the Pharisees were able to
accept the teachings of Jesus. Further, God will confront the
governments of the world with His laws and the governments
of the world will not be able to deal with the will of the Almighty within the limits of their constitutions. Confrontation
and consternation will face everyone. When Jesus came to
Earth the first time, He came to confront the best religion and
the strongest government the world had ever seen with His
truth. (Matthew 10:34) Neither could accommodate Jesus, but
there were individuals within these entities who received Him
as their Savior. To these believers, He gave the privilege of
being called "children of God." (John 1:12) Just before Jesus
appears the second time, the same will be true again. This
world and its organizations cannot receive Christ. He is alien.
His gospel and His ways are different. His truth and His law
stand in opposition to the religions and governments of men.
For Jesus to have complete dominion, men must let go of their
power and this loss will not come without a great struggle.
However, people who do choose to receive Him will be called
the "children of God."

Deuteronomy 13 – Part I – Prophets

Notice God's instructions to Moses in Deuteronomy 13: **"If a
prophet, or one who foretells by dreams, appears among
you and announces to you a miraculous sign or wonder,
and if the sign or wonder of which he has spoken takes**

place, and he says, 'Let us follow other gods' (gods you have not known) 'and let us worship them,' you must not listen to the words of that prophet or dreamer. The Lord your God is testing you to find out whether you love him with all your heart and with all your soul. It is the Lord your God you must follow, and him you must revere. Keep his commands and obey him; serve him and hold fast to him. That prophet or dreamer must be put to death, because he preached rebellion against the Lord your God, who brought you out of Egypt and redeemed you from the land of slavery; he has tried to turn you from the way the Lord your God commanded you to follow. You must purge the evil from among you. If your very own brother, or your son or daughter, or the wife you love, or your closest friend secretly entices you, saying, 'Let us go and worship other gods' (gods that neither you nor your fathers have known, gods of the peoples around you, whether near or far, from one end of the land to the other), do not yield to him or listen to him. Show him no pity. Do not spare him or shield him. You must certainly put him to death. Your hand must be the first in putting him to death, and then the hands of all the people. Stone him to death, because he tried to turn you away from the Lord your God, who brought you out of Egypt, out of the land of slavery. Then all Israel will hear and be afraid, and no one among you will do such an evil thing again. (Deuteronomy 13:1-11)

Deuteronomy 13 – Part II – Any Rise of New Doctrine

"If you hear it said about one of the towns the Lord your God is giving you to live in that wicked men have arisen among you and have led the people of their town astray, saying, 'Let us go and worship other gods' (gods you have not known), then you must inquire, probe and investigate it thoroughly. And if it is true and it has been proved that this detestable thing has been done among you, you must certainly put to the sword all who live in that town. Destroy it completely, both its people and its livestock. Gather all the plunder of the town into the middle of the public square and completely burn the town and all its plunder as a whole burnt offering to the Lord your God. It is to remain a ruin forever, never to be rebuilt. None of those condemned things shall be found in your hands, so that the Lord will turn from his fierce anger; he will show you mercy, have compassion on you, and increase your numbers, as he promised on oath to your forefathers, because you obey the Lord your God, keeping all his commands that I am giving you today and doing what is right in his eyes." (Deuteronomy 13:12-18)

Some people today read these and other verses within the Old Testament and conclude that the God of the Old Testament is not the God of the New Testament! In fact, people often present verses like these to demonstrate that the Old Testament had to be nailed to the cross. However, it is important to remember that these words *were given and meant to be applied* within the context of a theocracy – that is, during the time when God Himself ruled over Israel. God gave these instructions to Moses because no other gods would be tolerated as long as He ruled over Israel! Therefore, any deviation or allegiance to another god was an act of defiance against Jehovah. In this setting, it is understandable that total destruction was the only solution for open defiance against God. Unfortunately, the Pharisees in Saul's day presumed they were operating under the principles of a theocracy and they justified their actions toward the Christians with Scripture! The Jews thought they were doing God a service when they persecuted the Christians! (John 16:1-3)

Summary of Saul's Environment

This was the world Saul knew as a young man. The explosive growth of Christianity in Jerusalem became the focal point for increasing frustration of the Sanhedrin. Consequently, the Sanhedrin used Deuteronomy 13 as a basis for divine authority

(or so they thought) when dealing with dissident Christians.
As the drama unfolds, keep in mind the year is A.D. 34 and
Saul has just graduated from the school of the Pharisees. . . .

Stephen Condemned and Stoned

"So the word of God spread. The number of disciples in
Jerusalem increased rapidly, and a large number of
priests became obedient to the faith [and disobedient to
teachings of the Pharisees]. Now Stephen, a man full of
God's grace and power, did great wonders and miraculous signs among the people. Opposition arose, however,
from members of the Synagogue of the Freedmen (as it
was called) – Jews of Cyrene and Alexandria as well as
the provinces of Cilicia and Asia. These men began to
argue with Stephen, but they could not stand up
against his wisdom or the Spirit by whom he spoke.
Then they secretly persuaded some men to say, 'We have
heard Stephen speak words of blasphemy against Moses
and against God.' So they stirred up the people and the
elders and the teachers of the law [the Pharisees]. They
seized Stephen and brought him before the Sanhedrin.
They produced false witnesses, who testified, 'This
fellow never stops speaking against this holy place and
against the law. For we have heard him say that this
Jesus of Nazareth will destroy this place [Matthew 24:2]
and change the customs [the ceremonial system which]
Moses handed down to us.' All who were sitting in the
Sanhedrin looked intently at Stephen, and they saw
that his face was like the face of an angel. Then the high
priest asked him, 'Are these charges true?' " (Acts 6:7-
7:1, insertions mine)

The members of the Sanhedrin were well acquainted with the
disciples of Jesus, but Stephen was a new face. I believe this
incident occurred in the Spring of A.D. 34 during the week of
the Feast of Unleavened Bread. Jews from distant places like
Cyrene, Alexandria Egypt, the province of Cilicia and various
places in Asia had gathered in Jerusalem because of the re-

quired attendance for all Jews during Passover. (Exodus 34:24) In addition to this, the seventy weeks of Daniel 9 ended just 15 days earlier with the close of A.D. 33.

Somehow, Stephen and some of the visiting Jews became engaged in an aggressive religious discussion. When the Jews could not defeat the logic Stephen used from the Old Testament prophecies, they secretly schemed to have him arrested for dissension. When called before the Sanhedrin, Stephen was anxious to present Jesus to the leaders of Israel. Stephen explained why Jesus predicted the destruction of the temple by reviewing why the temple was necessary in the first place. He started with the call of Abraham, then the call of Moses and then the building of the temple by Solomon. (Acts 7:2-50) I believe Stephen was leading up to the point that Solomon's temple was only a temporary edifice until Messiah appeared. At that point, Messiah would be the temple and the focus of worship, instead of a physical edifice. (See Revelation 21:22.) Therefore, the destruction of the temple was appropriate because (a) bricks and mortar cannot house a God as great and majestic as Jehovah, and (b) Messiah had appeared. To underscore his point, Stephen quoted Isaiah 66:1,2, **"Heaven is my throne, and the earth is my footstool. What kind of house will you build for me? says the Lord. Or where will my resting place be? Has not my hand made all these things?"** (Acts 7:49,50)

Suddenly, Stephen stopped. He looked around at the 71 members of the Sanhedrin as the power and presence of the Holy Spirit came over him. Stephen was shown that his argument was useless, falling on deaf ears. He knew his death was imminent. The Holy Spirit gave Stephen words and the Spirit pronounced blood guilt upon Israel. **" 'You stiff-necked people, with uncircumcised hearts and ears! You are just like your fathers: You always resist the Holy Spirit! Was there ever a prophet your fathers did not persecute? They even killed those who predicted the coming of the Righteous One. And now you have betrayed and murdered him – you who have received the law that was**

put into effect through angels but have not obeyed it.'
When they heard this, they were furious and gnashed
their teeth at him. But Stephen, full of the Holy Spirit,
looked up to heaven and saw the glory of God, and
Jesus standing at the right hand of God. 'Look,' he said,
'I see heaven open and the Son of Man standing at the
right hand of God.' At this they covered their ears and,
yelling at the top of their voices, they all rushed at him,
dragged him out of the city and began to stone him.
Meanwhile, the witnesses laid their clothes at the feet of
a young man named Saul." (Acts 7:51-58)

Saul Persecutes The Church

Stephen was the first Christian martyr. He was the first
victim of an earlier decision the Sanhedrin had made to destroy all of the members of "The Way." Saul was an observer
in the courtroom when Stephen was tried. No doubt Saul was
gratified to see Stephen die, because he agreed with the
Sanhedrin that all Christians had to be destroyed or they
would destroy Judaism. As members of the Sanhedrin began
to shed their cloaks to stone Stephen, young Saul saw an
opportunity to be of service. He volunteered to hold the garments of the executioners – as I am sure he relished the excite-
ment of killing a Christian dissident.

"While they were stoning him, Stephen prayed, 'Lord
Jesus, receive my spirit.' Then he fell on his knees and
cried out, 'Lord, do not hold this sin against them.'
When he had said this, he fell asleep. And Saul was
there, giving approval to his death. On that day a great
persecution broke out against the church at Jerusalem,
and all except the apostles were scattered throughout
Judea and Samaria. Godly men buried Stephen and
mourned deeply for him." (Acts 7:59-8:2)

It is understandable that at that moment, Saul's heart was not
touched by the death of Stephen. Saul regarded Stephen as a
defiant dissident. For just such occasions, Jesus warned His
disciples about the blindness of religion, **"They will put you**

out of the synagogue; in fact, a time is coming when anyone who kills you will think he is offering a service to God. They will do such things because they have not known the Father or me. I have told you this, so that when the time comes you will remember that I warned you. I did not tell you this at first because I was with you." (John 16:2-4) Yet in Saul's mind, Deuteronomy 13 left no doubt that the Sanhedrin was doing the will of God. The stoning of Stephen was the fulfillment of what God required.

Saul seized the moment and used the destruction of Christians as a way to quickly advance himself within the Pharisee party. He volunteered to ferret out Christians and bring them before the Sanhedrin. The authorities were quite pleased that this young man was so willing to do the "dirty work." Saul was an ideologue (a person who follows an ideology in a dogmatic way without compromise), and was perfectly suited to implement Deuteronomy 13 to the letter of the law. The religious leaders gave Saul the necessary permits (to satisfy the Romans if anyone should care to ask) and the Bible says, ". . . Saul began to destroy the church. Going from house to house, he dragged off men and women and put them in prison. Those who had been scattered preached the word wherever they went." (Acts 8:3,4)

As a person might expect, the name, "Saul of Tarsus," quickly became infamous among Christians. Saul was fresh out of graduate school. He was bright and on a fast-track as far as his career in the party was concerned. He was devoted to legalism – always observing the letter of the law. He was so motivated that the suffering he inflicted on Christians did not bother him. He was willing to do what it took to save Judaism and his tireless actions made him perfect for the job.

Here is another end time parallel. During the Great Tribulation, many good people will commit the same kind of atrocities that Saul did, thinking they are doing a service for God. This parallel is important to understand, because when Stephen fell to his knees, he prayed, **"Lord, do not hold this sin against**

them." I find it interesting that these are among the final words of Jesus! **". . . Father, forgive them, for they do not know what they are doing."** (Luke 23:34) Why did Jesus and Stephen say these words when confronting death? I find one answer. When God steps into the affairs of man, there is confrontation. Truth meets blindness, but blindness does not know that it has confronted truth. Human ignorance and arrogance are such that a person with a good heart can do things that are offensive to God. "Good heart, wrong head." Both Jesus and Stephen knew there were a few good people who were sitting in judgment against them. They also knew that if people, like Gamaliel, who had honest hearts, could understand God's truth as they understood it, they would not be assaulting them. Instead, they would be standing with them. Therefore, both men expressed love for their enemies. They asked God to overlook the ignorance of their enemies because among their enemies they knew there were people with good hearts. Bible history proves that Saul was one such person!

Saul Meets Jesus

The more Saul chased the Christians throughout Jerusalem, the more the gospel spread as they fled for their lives! Eventually, Saul heard there were a significant number of Christians causing the same kind of problems in Damascus, so **". . . He went to the high priest and asked him for letters to the synagogues in Damascus, so that if he found any there who belonged to the Way, whether men or women, he might take them as prisoners to Jerusalem. As he neared Damascus on his journey, suddenly a light from heaven flashed around him. He fell to the ground and heard a voice say to him, 'Saul, Saul, why do you persecute me?' 'Who are you, Lord?' Saul asked. 'I am Jesus, whom you are persecuting,' he replied. 'Now get up and go into the city, and you will be told what you must do.' The men traveling with Saul stood there speechless; they heard the sound but did not see anyone. Saul got up from the ground, but when he opened his eyes he** could see nothing. So they led him by the hand into Damascus. For three days he was blind, and did not eat or drink anything." (Acts 9:1-9)

Saul was traveling to Damascus, intent on persecuting more Christians, when Jesus intercepted the young man by knocking him to the ground with a brilliant flash of light. After that brief encounter, Saul was left in a state of shock and totally blind. He did not know what to think or do. For the first time in his short but intense life, everything that Saul believed in, everything that he had studied, everything that he loved was suspect. Instead of the bright, self-directing, self-important and self-assured young Pharisee with a bright future, Saul was blind and totally confused. All he could think as he stumbled toward Damascus was, "So, Jesus Christ is God!" Saul arrived in Damascus in a very humble state, humiliated beyond words, and confused. Saul had come to Damascus to take Christians captive, but he arrived a prisoner of blindness. Saul was blind in more ways than one and for the first time in his life, he saw his blindness – a rare experience for anyone.

The Lights Come On

"In Damascus there was a disciple named Ananias. The Lord called to him in a vision, 'Ananias!' 'Yes, Lord,' he answered. The Lord told him, 'Go to the house of Judas on Straight Street and ask for a man from Tarsus named Saul, for he is praying. In a vision he has seen a man named Ananias come and place his hands on him to restore his sight.' 'Lord,' Ananias answered, 'I have heard many reports about this man and all the harm he has done to your saints in Jerusalem. And he has come here with authority from the chief priests to arrest all who call on your name.' But the Lord said to Ananias, 'Go! This man is my chosen instrument to carry my name before the Gentiles and their kings and before the people of Israel. I will show him how much he must suffer for my name.' Then Ananias went to the house and entered it. Placing his hands on Saul, he said,

"Brother Saul, the Lord – Jesus, who appeared to you on the road as you were coming here – has sent me so that you may see again and be filled with the Holy Spirit.' Immediately, something like scales fell from Saul's eyes, and he could see again. He got up and was baptized, and after taking some food, he regained his strength. Saul spent several days with the disciples in Damascus." (Acts 9:10-19)

The sincere words of Ananias touch my heart. He approached the young man and said kindly, "Brother Saul." Let me ask you a straight forward question. "What do you call your enemy? How do you address those who would do you harm? How do you respond to those who want to hurt you? Yet, Ananias said, "Brother Saul." The most amazing feature of true Christianity is the principle of "love your enemies." Nothing reveals the presence and power of God within a human being like the spirit of forgiveness. When a Christian holds no malice or hardness toward an adversary, the love of God radiates from that life. **"No one has ever seen God; but if we love one another, God lives in us and his love is made complete in us."** (1 John 4:12)

Saul had spent most of his life in school, preparing himself to be a Pharisee of the Pharisees. Now that he was in Damascus, Saul entered the first grade for a second time. This time he was studying Jesus instead of religion. Once his eyes were opened and his ears able to hear, Saul's new teachers were the ridiculed and *uneducated* disciples of Jesus.

Saul the Evangelist

After spending a week or two with the disciples, Saul was able to quickly align key elements from his formal education with his new spiritual eyesight and presto! Saul began to see that Jesus was the fulfillment of everything promised in the Old Testament. The young man was so excited he could not contain himself. Remember, all along he had a good heart, but his head was filled with wrong ideas. Now that Saul realized his blindness, his head could be directed toward truth. True to form, Saul was immediately ready to tell the whole world about Jesus! This is the amazing thing about people who are ideologues by nature. They are wholehearted and enthusiastic in everything they do. The Bible says of Saul:

"At once he began to preach in the synagogues that Jesus is the Son of God. All those who heard him were astonished and asked, 'Isn't he the man who raised havoc in Jerusalem among those who call on this name? And hasn't he come here to take them as prisoners to the chief priests?' Yet Saul grew more and more powerful and baffled the Jews living in Damascus by proving that Jesus is the Christ. After many days had gone by [about three years], the Jews conspired to kill him, but Saul learned of their plan. Day and night they kept close watch on the city gates in order to kill him. But his followers took him by night and lowered him in a basket through an opening in the wall." (Acts 9:20-25, insertion mine)

When the persecutor becomes the persecuted, it is apparent that an amazing change has taken place. Saul did not return to Jerusalem immediately after his conversion. The Holy Spirit called him to spend time in the solitude of the desert. Saul had much to unlearn, but he also had much to learn. He shared this experience with the Galatians because he wanted them to know that his understanding of the gospel came directly from Jesus Christ through the ministry of the Holy Sprit. His wrote, "For you have heard of my previous way of life in Judaism, how intensely I persecuted the church of God and tried to destroy it. I was advancing in Judaism beyond many Jews of my own age and was extremely zealous for the traditions of my fathers. But when God, who set me apart from birth and called me by his grace, was pleased to reveal his Son in me so that I might preach him among the Gentiles, I did not consult any man, nor did I go up to Jerusalem to see those who were apostles before I was, but I went immediately into [the desert of] Arabia and later returned to Damascus. **Then after three years, I went up to Jerusalem to get acquainted with Peter and stayed with him fifteen days.**" (Galatians 1:13-18, insertion mine)

Three years after leaving for Damascus, Saul returned to Jerusalem. Since there had not been any news about him and his whereabouts for such a long time, the disciples were not sure what he was up to. **"When he came to Jerusalem, he tried to join the disciples, but they were all afraid of him, not believing that he really was a disciple. But Barnabas took him and brought him to the apostles. He told them how Saul on his journey had seen the Lord and that the Lord had spoken to him, and how in Damascus he had preached fearlessly in the name of Jesus. So Saul stayed with them and moved about freely in Jerusalem, speaking boldly in the name of the Lord. He talked and debated with the Grecian Jews, but they tried to kill him. When the brothers learned of this, they took him down to Caesarea and sent him off to Tarsus. Then the church throughout Judea, Galilee and Samaria enjoyed a time of peace. It was strengthened; and encouraged by the Holy Spirit, it grew in numbers, living in the fear of the Lord."** (Acts 9: 26-31)

Summary

The limits of space do not allow me to present the marvelous life of Saul beyond this point. Therefore, I will close with a review of some of the end time parallels that can be found in Saul's life:

1. During the Great Tribulation, the religious leaders of the world will parallel the behavior of the Pharisees and the Sadducees. Conservatives, like the Pharisees of old, will insist that the only way to appease God so that His judgments might stop is by rigorous obedience. The problem is that their idea of how to appease God will be faulty. There is an obedience that stems from legalism (the carnal heart) and there is an obedience that springs from faith (the spiritual heart). The question is not whether God requires

obedience, the question is whether our obedience springs from faith and love! Liberals, like the Sadducees of old, will use their political connections and influence civil powers to produce legislation that attempts to control and thwart the 144,000. As in Paul's day, when Pharisees and Sadducees united against the apostles and early Christians, so in the end times, conservatives and liberals will unite against the testimony of God's 144,000 and end time Christians.

2. After Jesus went to Heaven, He gave His disciples two great powers. First, He gave them words and wisdom to speak for God. Jesus promised, **"But when they arrest you, do not worry about what to say or how to say it. At that time you will be given what to say, for it will not be you speaking, but the Spirit of your Father speaking through you."** (Matthew 10:19,20) Second, He gave the disciples Holy Spirit power and enabled them to perform hundreds of genuine miracles. Jesus promised, **"But you will receive power when the Holy Spirit comes on you; and you will be my witnesses in Jerusalem, and in all Judea and Samaria, and to the ends of the Earth."** (Acts 1:8) God granted them miracle working powers so that people would listen to the testimony of the disciples, believe, be "born again," and then spread the message abroad. These two gifts rested upon Paul and Barnabas as well. **"So Paul and Barnabas spent considerable time there [Iconium], speaking boldly for the Lord, who confirmed the message of his grace by enabling them to do miraculous signs and wonders."** (Acts 14:3, insertion mine) This same process will happen again. God will give His 144,000 servants words and wisdom to speak for Him. They will clearly present the terms and conditions of salvation from the Scriptures and the power of the Holy Spirit will rest upon them, enabling them to perform *genuine* miracles on demand. These two gifts are described in Revelation 11 as the Two Witnesses.

3. The love of religion is blinding, so it is impossible for one man to prove the superiority of his religion over that of another. A devout Christian cannot *prove* to a devout Jew that his or her religion is superior to Judaism. History confirms this. Jesus could not *prove* to the Jews that He was Messiah! Jesus could not prove to His disciples that He was Messiah, either! One day, Jesus asked Peter if he believed that He was the Son of God and Peter responded "Yes." Jesus then said, **"Blessed are you, Simon son of Jonah, for this was not revealed to you by man, but by my Father in Heaven."** (Matthew 16:17) Given the onerous power of religion, let me ask – what were the chances of young Saul abandoning Judaism and accepting Christianity after listening to Stephen's testimony? Zero. In fact, Saul was so convinced of the accuracy of his religious position that miracles and reasoning from Scripture could not make a dent in his thinking. The same was true of the Pharisees and Sadducees during the days of Jesus. They saw Jesus perform miracles with their own eyes and the evidence of His work was everywhere. Yet, the only thing they could say was **". . . By Beelzebub, the prince of demons, he is driving out demons."** (Luke 11:15) During the Great Tribulation, God will tear down the walls of religion with a marvelous display of power and *open* the eyes of everyone on Earth to truth for a short time. God will confront humankind with powerful manifestations of truth and power. He will force everyone to make a decision for truth or against truth. The honest in heart, like Saul, will see the light – discover their blindness and rejoice! People who love religion and power, like the Pharisees and Sadducees, will align themselves with darkness to survive, but will forfeit eternal life. The experience of Saul on the road to Damascus has an end time parallel. Many people on Earth have honest hearts, but wrong heads. At the appointed time, God will allow everyone to see the light. All who receive the truth, like Saul, will be found among that greater number of saints when they go marching in.

4. The Bible does not tell us how or when Saul's name was changed to Paul. Luke simply identifies Saul was as the one who is also called Paul. **"Then Saul, who was also called Paul, filled with the Holy Spirit, looked straight at Elymas and said, 'You are a child of the devil and an enemy of everything that is right! You are full of all kinds of deceit and trickery. Will you never stop perverting the right ways of the Lord?' "** (Acts 13:9,10) I can almost hear the apostle Paul saying these words – given the fact that he, too, perverted the right ways of the Lord! Although it does not really matter how Saul became known as Paul, I have a possible explanation for you to consider. When the Lord informed Saul that he would become an apostle to the Gentiles, (1 Timothy 2:7) I conclude that Saul converted his Jewish name to a Gentile equivalent, so they would accept him more readily. (The Jews were intensely hated throughout the Roman Empire and very few Gentiles would listen to a despised Jew. See Acts 16:20.) Even more, a new identity reflects a new life. (Saul abandoned the Pharisees and I am sure the feeling was mutual.) The apostle Paul had one objective. He wanted everyone to know Christ and the joy of His salvation. He wrote the following: **"Though I am free and belong to no man, I make myself a slave to everyone, to win as many as possible. To the Jews I became like a Jew, to win the Jews. To those under the law I became like one under the law (though I myself am not under the law), so as to win those under the law. To those [Gentiles] not having the law I became like one not having the law (though I am not free from God's law but am under Christ's law), so as to win those not having the law. To the weak I became weak, to win the weak. I have become all things to all men so that by all possible means I might save some. I do all this for the sake of the gospel, that I may share in its blessings."** (1 Corinthians 9:12-23, insertion mine)

History says that Paul was executed in Rome around A.D. 65 for refusing to worship Caesar. He fought a good fight and he was faithful to the end. (2 Timothy 4:7) After studying Paul's writings and his life of service for the Lord Jesus Christ, I am forever indebted to this zealous man for showing me many wonderful things about Jesus. Jesus halted Saul on the road to Damascus because he was totally dedicated to the service of God (albeit, misdirected). What is so wonderful about God is that He sees the heart! He knew that once Saul met Jesus, his life would be forever changed. Paul wrote 14 of the 27 books found in the New Testament! Where would Christians be without his contribution to the Bible? Paul's life is a perfect example of a complete paradigm shift. What he used to love, he came to hate and what he used to hate, he came to love. **"But whatever was to my profit I now consider loss for the sake of Christ. What is more, I consider everything a loss compared to the surpassing greatness of knowing Christ Jesus my Lord, for whose sake I have lost all things. I consider them** [my losses] **rubbish, that I may gain Christ and be found in him, not having a righteousness of my own that comes from the law, but that which is through faith in Christ – the righteousness that comes from God and is by faith."** (Philippians 3:7-9, insertion mine) May God help each of us to emulate the integrity, love, humility and dedication demonstrated in the life of a dear saint who became known as Paul.

Chapter 7

John the Baptizer

In the previous chapter, we found several end time parallels in the story of Elijah. I think it is fitting that we examine John the Baptists life after studying Elijah, because John and Elijah have several things in common. For example, when it came to speaking boldly against sin, both men were singularly notorious in their day. Both men challenged an apostate church-state system. Both men rose out of obscurity. Both men grew up in the desert wilderness. Both men were not formally educated nor were any of their writings preserved for us to read. Exceptional Holy Spirit power filled both men and God granted both of them the honor of seeing Jesus with their own eyes!

Some people confuse John the Baptist with the apostle John. They are not the same person. John the Baptist was six months older than Jesus and about ten or twelve years older than the apostle John. The apostle John wrote the Gospel of John, three epistles that bear his name and the Book of Revelation, whereas John the Baptist wrote none of the books found in the Bible.

John's birth (like that of Isaac) was a miraculous event because his parents were of an advanced age. The Bible record indicates that John's father was a Levite priest named Zachariah and his mother's name was Elizabeth. Like the prophet Jeremiah, God chose John, gave him a name, and ordained him as a prophet *before* he was even born! (Jeremiah 1:5; Luke 1:13-17) Even more, Jesus selected John to be His forerunner before either of them were born! To stretch your mind even further, Jesus not only chose Mary and Joseph as His parents, but He also chose Zachariah and Elizabeth to be John's parents. Because Zachariah and Elizabeth were too old to have children, John's miracle birth gave added credibility to his message when he began his ministry and became known as the Baptizer.

John was born in the hill country of Judea, but he spent most of his life in the solitude of the desert wilderness. Evidently, his elderly parents died when he was a young man. As in the life of Moses, the wilderness prepared John for his difficult mission. John carefully studied the Scriptures as the Holy Spirit led him to understand many prophecies in the Old Testament that pointed to the appearing of Messiah and the establishment of His kingdom. John discovered that Messiah would appear *at the beginning* of the seventieth week, which is mentioned in Daniel 9. Therefore, in the Spring of A.D. 27, at the beginning of the seventieth week of seven years, John began proclaiming *the year had come* for the Messiah to appear and He would establish His kingdom shortly. (Matthew 3:2,11; Luke 3; also Jesus' comments in Mark 1:15; Luke 4:18,19) Of course, the Jews ridiculed John for his beliefs, but many of them listened to John and believed his testimony. There is no record of John the Baptist ever performing any miracles, but many people still regarded him as a prophet of God. (Matthew 14:5)

The Ritual of Baptism

There is an interesting history behind John's title, "John the Baptist." Of course, the title, "the Baptist," was not part of John's name at birth nor was he a member of the Baptist Church, as some Christians naively believe. John lived and died as a Jew. He was among the few in Israel who believed Jesus was the long awaited Messiah. When John began his public ministry, he became notorious for doing something considered very strange. John insisted on baptizing *Jews* in the Jordan River. Typically, Jews were not the ones baptized, because they were the descendants of Abraham *by birth.* Conversely, they baptized the Gentiles as "a pledge of allegiance" when they wished to become sons of Abraham. (Few Gentiles converted to Judaism in those days, so baptisms by the priests were scarce. Matthew 23:15)

The Jews regarded a Gentile's baptism as both a mystical and a practical experience. In a mystical sense, the Jews believed a Gentile's past was "washed away" when he or she was immersed. Emerging from the water, the person became a new son or daughter of Abraham! Today, baptism, like the marriage ceremony, is a public declaration. In baptism, you demonstrate your allegiance to God and to the principles of His kingdom before witnesses. In marriage, you state your allegiance to your spouse before witnesses. Even though the origin of baptism is uncertain, baptism symbolized to Israel its experience as a nation. When God delivered Israel from Egypt (the old life of slavery), they had to pass through the waters of the Jordan River (immersed in the river) and when they emerged from the water, they inherited the promised land (the birth of a new nation). When the Jews baptized a Gentile, they *adopted* him into one of the twelve tribes and they entered the date of his baptism into the genealogical records of Israel.

When John began preaching that Messiah was about to appear and set up His kingdom, John insisted that baptism was a necessary pledge of allegiance. In effect, John was preaching that Jews, yes Jews, needed to convert to *a new and better* religion – a religion centered on the worship of Messiah instead of the slaughter of animals. (The old religion of slaughtering animals was about to disappear.) John understood that salvation from sin required an atonement which animals could not satisfy. When Jesus appeared on the banks of the Jordan River in the Fall of A.D. 27 for baptism, the Holy Spirit gave John utterance and he cried out, **"Behold the Lamb of God that taketh away the sin of the world!"** (John 1:29, KJV)

Why Was Jesus Baptized?

Many people are puzzled that Jesus asked John to baptize Him. Did Jesus need to have His sins washed away? No. Jesus never sinned. (Hebrews 4:15) Did Jesus need to repent of rebellion against His Father in Heaven? No. Jesus and the Father are one in spirit and truth. (John 10:30) Did Jesus have to be born again? No. Jesus did not have a carnal nature. (Colossians 2:9) Then why did Jesus request to be baptized?

Jesus submitted Himself to be baptized by John for two reasons. First, Jesus was born "under law" (Galatians 4:4) and He was subject to the Levitical system He was about to end. (Hebrews 7)

By His death on the cross, Jesus terminated the entire Levitical system. After His resurrection, Jesus planned to establish a new world order on Earth and a new kingdom based on a new and much better covenant. At just the right time, John appeared in the desert proclaiming the arrival of Messiah and His coming kingdom. John's call to be baptized was an invitation to be part of the new order; it was a pledge of allegiance. *Jesus submitted to John's baptism to declare His loyalty to the principles of His coming kingdom.* This is a profound point about the character of God. The Omniscient Creator of the Universe, is subject to His own laws. Jesus is not arbitrary nor dictatorial. If He were, God would be inconsistent and chaos would fill the universe. God loves order and where there is moral order, there is a rule of law.

Jesus told the timid Nicodemus, "**. . . I tell you the truth, no one can enter the kingdom of God unless he is born of water and the Spirit.**" (John 3:5) Some people distort the words of Jesus to mean that unless a person is baptized he or she cannot be saved. This is not so. Many circumstances can prevent a person from being baptized. For instance, the thief on the cross was not baptized in his final moments of life, yet he sincerely surrendered his life to Jesus and the Lord Himself assured him of salvation. Furthermore, the Bible clearly teaches that works or rituals do not save us. (Ephesians 2:8,9) We are saved through our faith in Jesus. When a person lives by faith, he or she is willing to go, to be and to do all that God asks, without compromise. A life of faith is demonstrated by a loyal life. However, even if a person is baptized, it does not necessarily guarantee salvation. (Matthew 7:20-23) Baptism – like marriage vows – is a public declaration of loyalty and God requires it for our benefit! Public declarations provide a way to tell others who we are and what we stand for.

For the person who believes in Christ, baptism symbolizes the death and burial of their carnal nature and the resurrection of a new person controlled by a spiritual nature. (John 3 and Matthew 28) Paul elaborates on the beauty of this concept in Romans 6-8. In submitting to John's baptism, Jesus declared His loyalty to the principles of God's coming kingdom. God loves order and where there is order, there is law.

Second, *Jesus was baptized because He does not ask His followers to do something that He has not done first. He is our example.* Remember, Jesus stooped to wash the feet of His disciples and He commanded them to do the same to each other. **"If I then, your Lord and Master, have washed your feet; ye also ought to wash one another's feet. For I have given you an example, that ye should do as I have done to you. Verily, verily, I say unto you, The servant is not greater than his lord; neither he that is sent greater than he that sent him."** (John 13:14-16) Jesus chose baptism, not because He had a carnal past to wash away, but to give us an example of stepping out of our inherited religion and joining in His inheritance! Jesus affirmed with His baptism that everyone – Jew and Gentile alike – must declare allegiance to the kingdom of God. Baptism is a public declaration of one's loyalty to God and the principles of His kingdom! Baptism is to God's people what the mark of the beast will be for those who worship the Antichrist during the Great Tribulation.

Just before Jesus returned to Heaven, He told His disciples, **"Therefore go and make disciples of all nations, baptizing them in the name of the Father and of the Son and of the Holy Spirit, and teaching them to obey everything I have commanded you. And surely I am with you always, to the very end of the age."** (Matthew 28:19,20) In a practical way, baptism is *an event* that separates yesterday from tomorrow. Baptism declares severance – the old life is over and a new life has begun. Baptism should reflect an inner transformation – from unbeliever to believer – from a carnal person to a spiritual person – from dominion by the sinful nature to dominion by the spiritual nature – from being a part of this world to being a part of the world to come.

King James Translators

Because of his urgent message and his strange insistence that *Jews* be baptized into the coming kingdom of God, John the

Baptist became known in the Greek language as "John, the one who immerses." The Greek word *baptizo* means to immerse or dunk. At the beginning of the seventeenth century, the meaning of *baptizo* presented a problem for the translators of the King James version of the Bible. Most Christians did not practice baptism by immersion in the seventeenth century. Instead, the ceremony of baptism came to mean the sprinkling of water, most often, the sprinkling of infants soon after birth.

(**Note:** The Church of Rome concluded around the third century A.D. that a person could not be saved unless he or she underwent the ritual of baptism. Since infant mortality was very high in those days, the practice of infant baptism became necessary to insure that all children would be saved. Centuries later, many Protestants carried this doctrine with them when they left the Catholic Church.)

The translators realized they could not translate the Greek word *baptizo* as immersing or dunking without causing a big theological problem for the king, so they chose to transliterate *baptizo* rather than translate it. By placing the English word "baptize" in the Bible without explaining the meaning as the act of immersing or dunking, everyone could interpret baptism as he thought best. The translators also transliterated John's title to "John the Baptist" instead of "John, the one who immerses."

First End Time Parallel

There are some important end time parallels associated with John the Baptist. First, the role John the Baptist played as the First Advent approached will be the same role the 144,000 will fulfill as the Second Advent approaches. As we continue to examine John's ministry, please keep this in mind. During the Great Tribulation, God will use 144,000 "baptizing Johns" to announce the timely appearing of the King of kings and the Lord of lords and the establishment of His kingdom! The 144,000 will come from every race, language, religion and nation. Assuming there are six billion people on Earth when the Great Tribulation begins, the ratio of God's servants to the population of Earth will be approximately one per 50,000 people. Assuming God's servants are evenly distributed over the world during the Great Tribulation, China would have about 29,000 of the 144,000, India would have about 28,000 of the 144,000 and the United States would have about 7,000 servants of God. Of course, God will insure that every nation has enough "baptizing Johns" to accomplish the gospel commission during the Great Tribulation.

Elijah-type People

Notice the words of Malachi: **"See, I will send you the prophet Elijah before that great and dreadful day of the Lord comes. He will turn the hearts of the fathers to their children, and the hearts of the children to their fathers; or else I will come and strike the land with a curse."** (Malachi 4:5,6) The prophet Malachi gave this prophecy about 350 years before the birth of Jesus. Jewish leaders during the time of Christ were not certain of its meaning, but they did know two things. First, they knew that God took Elijah to Heaven in a fiery chariot (2 Kings 2). Second, they knew that the great and dreadful day of the Lord was still in the future. (Joel 2, Obadiah 1, Isaiah 13 and Ezekiel 30) The Jews in Christ's day believed that the great and dreadful day of the Lord came in a two-part installment. The *great part* would be their exaltation as a nation and the *dreadful part* would be the destruction of their enemies – which by inference were God's enemies. This was the egocentric mind set of the Jewish leaders regarding Malachi 4 when John the Baptist began to preach in the desert.

Many people were drawn to the wilderness to hear John's compelling message because he spoke with unusual clarity and penetrating power. His preaching brought hope, but it also caused fear. When he preached about the imminent appearing of the Messiah, John's careful explanation of the prophecies brought hope to the hopeless. When he preached about God's love and His willingness to save sinners, there was joy. However, when he preached about God's wrath toward sin, John's sobering words caused people to reflect seriously on their lives. This often caused fear to fill the hearts of the people present. They listened and asked, "Who was worthy to receive God's salvation?" The Holy Spirit's presence and power gave John's words depth and scorching relevance. *All people who listened to John felt the unseen, but obvious presence of the Holy Spirit* – it could be compared with the experience of standing in the authoritative presence of Elijah on Mount Carmel. With this compelling power and the evidence of Scripture to back his words, John warned men and women to repent or be destroyed. The options were simple. John insisted upon heartfelt repentance, full restitution and baptism for everyone. There could be no love for sin in the coming kingdom of God.

One day, after preaching to a large crowd, John began to answer questions. Notice his answers:

"The ax is already at the root of the trees, and every tree that does not produce good fruit will be cut down and thrown into the fire. 'What should we do then?' the crowd asked. John answered, 'The man with two tunics should share with him who has none, and the one who has food should do the same.' Tax collectors also came to be baptized. 'Teacher,' they asked, 'what should we do?' 'Don't collect any more than you are required to,' he told them. Then some soldiers asked him, 'And what should we do?' He replied, 'Don't extort money and don't accuse people falsely – be content with your pay.' " (Luke 3:9-14)

John taught that God's kingdom would coexist with a world of evil kingdoms for a time. Eventually, there would be a purified Earth. I can think of at least three reasons why John's message was believable. First, it was based on Scripture. Second, John's message was timely. He showed from the prophecies that the time had come for the appearing of Messiah. Third, the Holy Spirit gave John's words great power, clarity and effectiveness. If a person listened, he or she could not help but be moved – either into submission or rejection. One day, some scribes and Pharisees came, presented themselves before John and asked him to baptize them – just in case John's predictions might come true. Of course, they had no intention of humbling themselves to do what John was proclaiming and be right in God's sight. The Holy Spirit enabled John to see their pretense and his response was harsh. "... **You brood of vipers! Who warned you to flee from the coming wrath** [of God]?" (Matthew 3:7, insertion mine)

God's Timing

Let there be no mistake – the appearing of John the Baptist was a prophetic fulfillment. His single purpose – assigned before birth – was to prepare people for the coming of the Lord, Jesus Christ. The appearing of John the Baptist should have put the priests on notice that Messiah was not far behind! For centuries, the Jews had discussed the promise of a Deliverer and in John's day, the promise was so old that many people had begun to question its truthfulness, as if God had forgotten! At the time of John, the nation of Israel was in trouble because Rome had removed Archelaus, the son of wicked Herod, and many Jews had died during the revolt. The iron hand of Rome rested heavy upon the neck of Israel. The Romans occupied Jerusalem and the occupation provoked their mutual hatred of each other. This tiny tribal Jewish nation, within the vast Roman empire, desperately needed a Savior.

Then came John. Imagine the interest he aroused when he began to preach about the imminent appearing of the Savior. The Bible says, **"The people were waiting expectantly and were all wondering in their hearts if John might possibly be the Christ."** (Luke 3:15) At this moment in history, people were filled with expectancy. This expectancy soared as John explained Daniel 9 to his audiences. Daniel 9 predicted that the Messiah would appear in the 484th year after the decree to restore and rebuild Jerusalem. (Daniel 9:25) John explained how 69 weeks had expired since the decree of Artaxerxes to rebuild Jerusalem (457 B.C.). Therefore the actual year for the appearing of Messiah had come and God would establish His kingdom soon afterwards. Many Jews began seriously to consider the possibility of John being the Messiah.

The number of people visiting the wilderness to see John continued to escalate. Concerned, the Sanhedrin sent a deputation of priests to investigate this mysterious man and his message.

Note their words: **"Now this was John's testimony when
the Jews of Jerusalem sent priests and Levites to ask
him who he was. He did not fail to confess, but confessed
freely, 'I am not the Christ.' They asked him, 'Then who
are you? Are you Elijah?' He said, 'I am not.' 'Are you the
Prophet** [predicted by Moses]**?' He answered, 'No.' Finally
they said, 'Who are you? Give us an answer to take back
to those who sent us. What do you say about yourself?'
John replied in the words of Isaiah the prophet, 'I am the
voice of one calling in the desert, Make straight the way
for the Lord.' "** (John 1:19-23, insertion mine) Did you notice
the order of their questions? Did you notice who the priests
were expecting? What they believed about Malachi's prophecy
prompted their questions.

Why Must Elijah Appear?

Israel's religious leaders talked openly and frequently about the
coming of Elijah, although verifying Elijah's identity was always the subject of many discussions. For example, they wondered how they could distinguish someone who may be masquerading as Elijah from the true Elijah, especially if the false
Elijah performed miracles? Would Elijah come down from
Heaven in a fiery chariot? Would Elijah appear in the body of a
human being? If Elijah came as an ordinary man, how could
they positively identify him?

After Peter, James and John had seen Jesus on the mount of
transfiguration, they had positive proof that Jesus was the
Messiah, the Son of God. They were anxious to share what they
had seen, but Jesus forbade them to reveal this information
until after His resurrection. He knew that these claims from His
disciples would limit His effectiveness among the Jews. (Matthew 17:9) But, the transfiguration of Jesus did raise a prophetic issue. The disciples wondered why Elijah had not appeared, since this is what Malachi predicted. The disciples knew
that John the Baptist was not Elijah. John had clearly denied
he was Elijah. Trying to reconcile the transfiguration experience of Jesus with the prophecy of Malachi, they asked the
Master, **". . . 'Why then do the teachers of the law say that**

Elijah must come first?' Jesus replied, 'To be sure, Elijah
comes and will restore all things. But I tell you, Elijah
has already come, and they did not recognize him, but
have done to him everything they wished. In the same
way the Son of Man is going to suffer at their hands.'
Then the disciples understood that he was talking to
them about John the Baptist." (Matthew 17:10-12)

These verses contain more substance than most people realize.
First, Jesus affirms the validity of Malachi's prophecy saying,
"To be sure, Elijah comes and will restore all things."
Then, Jesus said, **"Elijah has already come and they did
not recognize him."** Even though the disciples understood
that Jesus was speaking about John the Baptist, they were still
puzzled. They had just seen Moses and Elijah, yet Jesus was
saying that John the Baptist was Elijah. Here is the problem:

If You Are Willing to Accept It . . .

A few months before the transfiguration of Jesus occurred, King
Herod had arrested and imprisoned John the Baptist because
John had offended him. The arrogant king had taken his
brother's wife, Herodias, to be his own and John the Baptist told
Herod that he had committed a grievous sin. Of course, Herod
did not want to hear the truth and Herodias was shamed.
Herod was so furious with John that he wanted John killed.
However, Herod was not stupid. He knew that the people regarded John as a prophet and Herod did not want to jeopardize
his position as king by starting another Jewish uprising that
might reach the ears of Caesar.

So, Herod did the next best thing and put John in prison. From
the silence of his prison cell, John began to reflect on his life's
mission, his teachings and beliefs. Yes, Jesus had appeared
right on time and Jesus had begun His ministry just as John
had predicted. Yet, he could not understand why Jesus had not
declared Himself to be the Messiah, nor had He done anything
to establish the kingdom of God! In the darkness of that prison
cell, it did not seem to John like events were unfolding as the
Scriptures predicted. Lonely, cold and troubled, John began to

question some of his beliefs and his ministry. When some of his disciples came to visit, he asked them to ask Jesus a pointed question.

"When John heard in prison what Christ was doing, he sent his disciples to ask him, 'Are you the one who was to come, or should we expect someone else?' Jesus replied, 'Go back and report to John what you hear and see: The blind receive sight, the lame walk, those who have leprosy are cured, the deaf hear, the dead are raised, and the good news is preached to the poor. Blessed is the man who does not fall away on account of me.' " (Matthew 11:2-6) Jesus answered John's question with veiled language. He knew John was a keen student of the Scriptures, and so Jesus answered John's disciples with words from Isaiah 61. He also knew that His affirming response would give John the assurance he needed to believe that Jesus was the Messiah. Other people who were present had no idea that Jesus' response was affirming that He was the Messiah. Jesus knew it was not time to make this public disclosure. In fact, it was Jesus' desire to keep this fact hidden until He was resurrected, knowing that premature promotion of His identity would thwart His mission. (Matthew 17:9)

"As John's disciples were leaving, Jesus began to speak to the crowd about John: 'What did you go out into the desert to see? A reed swayed by the wind? If not, what did you go out to see? A man dressed in fine clothes? No, those who wear fine clothes are in kings' palaces. Then what did you go out to see? A prophet? Yes, I tell you, and more than a prophet. *This is the one about whom it is written:* **"I will send my messenger ahead of you, who will prepare your way before you."** **I tell you the truth: Among those born of women there has not** *risen anyone greater than John the Baptist***; yet he who is least in the kingdom of heaven is greater than he. From the days of John the Baptist until now, the kingdom of heaven has been forcefully advancing, and forceful men lay hold of it. For all the Prophets and the Law** [the Scriptures]

prophesied until [about the appearing of] **John. And if you are willing to accept it, he is the Elijah who was to come.'"** (Matthew 11:7-14, insertions and italics mine)

In response to John's request, Jesus quoted Malachi 3:1. In this passage, it indicates that God would send a messenger to announce the appearing of Messiah, and Jesus was assuring John the Baptist that he was that messenger. Jesus clearly told the crowd that John was "the Elijah to come." However, Jesus phrased His declaration in an interesting way, **"if you are willing to accept it. . . ."** Why did Jesus say it this way? Jesus had been on Earth long enough to know that "the great day of the Lord" mentioned in Malachi 4 was not going to happen during His lifetime on Earth. In fact, Jesus knew that establishing His kingdom on Earth would not be possible. Said another way, Jesus was saying to His disciples, *if you can accept this by faith, John the Baptist would have been the fulfillment of Malachi 4:5,6 if the nation of Israel had been faithful to the terms and conditions set forth in Daniel 9!*

"Plan A" – "Plan B"

The fulfillment of Malachi 4:5,6 is inseparably connected to "the great day of the Lord." Since "the great day of the Lord" has not happened, some people believe Malachi 4:5,6 still awaits fulfillment. I do not believe this is the case. If you can accept the following two statements, there is a simple explanation for the prophecy of Malachi 4:5,6:

1. Israel knew the redemptive conditions outlined in the 70 weeks prophecy of Daniel 9. If they had met these conditions, the plan of salvation and "the great day of the Lord" would have been completed long ago. All of the Old Testament prophecies given by Isaiah, Jeremiah, Joel, Amos, Ezekiel, Malachi and others would have been fulfilled just *as they were written.* "The great day of the Lord" would have happened shortly after the end of the seventieth week if Israel had met the conditions God set forth in Daniel 9. In other words, if Israel had satisfied these conditions, John the Baptist would have fulfilled the prophecy of Malachi 4 to the letter and that would have been the end of the story.

2. Since Israel failed, God's plan for Israel and the establishment of His kingdom on Earth was not implemented at the end of the seventieth week – simply put, Israel rejected the Messiah. This is a profound point: A person must have a Messiah's heart to accept the teachings and truths taught by the Messiah. For this reason, we must be born again. Most of the people in Israel rejected and crucified the Messiah because they did not have a Messiah's heart. The character and principles of the Messiah's kingdom were foreign to the people of Israel and they rejected Him. Because God's original plan could not be fulfilled, the prophecies of the Old Testament ("Plan A") **were made null and void**. To keep His promise and the covenant He made with Abraham, God made several changes. First, He redefined Israel. Everyone who now receives Christ is an heir of Abraham. In Christ, racial origin has no meaning. (Galatians 3:28,29) Second, Jesus raised up new trustees of the gospel. These trustees became known as Christians. (Matthew 28:19,20; Acts 11:26) Third, God established a new prophetic schematic that is found in the book of Revelation. I call this a new course of action "Plan B." There are many parallels between "Plan A" and "Plan B," **but** these parallels are separate and distinct. One cannot merge "Plan A" events into a "Plan B" schematic. For example, under "Plan A," Messiah would have governed His kingdom from the City of David, e.g., Jerusalem. Under "Plan B" Jesus will govern His kingdom from His throne in *New* Jerusalem. (Revelation 22:3) The point is that the appearing of Elijah, predicted in Malachi 3 and 4, was connected to "the great day of the Lord" which was supposed to happen soon after the first advent of Messiah. However, after the Jews rejected Christ, God scrapped "Plan A" due to Israel's failure to meet the conditions placed upon them in Daniel 9. However, a parallel of Malachi's prophecy remains. The parallel ("Plan B") is found in Revelation 7. The heralds that will appear before "the great day of the Lord" will be 144,000 servants of God!

The Spirit and Power of Elijah

Notice what the angel said about John the Baptist before his birth. **"But the angel said to him: 'Do not be afraid, Zechariah; your prayer has been heard. Your wife Elizabeth will bear you a son, and you are to give him the name John. He will be a joy and delight to you, and many will rejoice because of his birth, for he will be great in the sight of the Lord.** *He is never to take wine or other fermented drink*, **and he will be filled with the Holy Spirit even from birth. Many of the people of Israel will he bring back to the Lord their God. And he will go on before the Lord, in the spirit and power of Elijah, to turn the hearts of the fathers to their children and the disobedient to the wisdom of the righteous – to make ready a people prepared for the Lord.' "** (Luke 1:13-17, italics mine) It is interesting that God forbade this all-important herald of Jesus from drinking anything that would alter his mind. God's servants must be filled with the Holy Spirit, not a bottle of spirits.

God gave John the spirit and power of Elijah so he could *turn* the hearts of fathers toward their children and the disobedient toward the wisdom of the righteous – to make a group of people ready for the Lord's coming. How did John do this? John's message explained God's love for sinners, but simultaneously called sin by its right name. John condemned fathers for bringing children into the world, only to shirk their God-given responsibility to be a loving father and a noble mentor for their children. John also condemned fathers and mothers for their spiritual neglect. John used Israel's history of apostasy to prove how nations degenerate rapidly, especially if parents do not teach and demonstrate to their children the importance of loving and obeying God. Fathers had been lax about being spiritual role models and they had neglected to maintain the family altar. Furthermore, they had abdicated their parental responsibilities to religious schools and others. The Holy Spirit's powerful conviction fell upon those who listened. Many fathers repented of their sins, transformed their ways and were baptized! Remember, John was not conducting a baptismal campaign and counting heads. He was preaching a life-transforming gospel that bore fruit and baptism by John was a pledge of allegiance.

John did not neglect to speak to the youth, either. After all, John was a single young man himself – only 30 years of age. As young people listened, the boldness and penetration of his message impressed them. John minced no words when he pointed out that most youth were unfit to participate in the coming kingdom of God. Their rebellion against their parents and teachers made them essentially worthless for the purposes of God. John was firm, but kind. John used the circumstances surrounding his own birth to impress young people that God had a purpose for each life, but that purpose could be fulfilled only when God had dominion in the heart. He reminded the youth that God did not agree with their focus on pleasure and the acquisition of money. John's abstemious life in the desert reflected a high calling, and I am sure he asked, "Where are those willing to forsake the world and serve God?"

Malachi 4 and Revelation 7

The parallel between the promise of Elijah ("Plan A") and the appearing of the 144,000 ("Plan B") awaits fulfillment. Revelation reveals the identity of Elijah for our generation! Revelation reveals there will be 144,000 servants of God who will have the spirit and power of Elijah. This is the *next* prophetic event. Revelation also tells us that God is holding back the four winds of His wrath until His Elijah servants are prepared and ready to do their work. Revelation also reveals that God will empower the Elijah messengers for 1,260 days. Most (if not all) of the 144,000 will be martyrs for Christ, just as John the Baptist became a martyr for the cause of Christ. The martyrdom of John brings up a good point. Notice the text:

"Now Herod had arrested John and bound him and put him in prison because of Herodias, his brother Philip's wife, for John had been saying to him: 'It is not lawful for you to have her.' Herod wanted to kill John, but he

was afraid of the people, because they considered him a prophet. On Herod's birthday the daughter of Herodias danced for them and pleased Herod so much that he promised with an oath to give her whatever she asked. Prompted by her mother, she said, 'Give me here on a platter the head of John the Baptist.' The king was distressed, but because of his oaths and his dinner guests, he ordered that her request be granted and had John beheaded in the prison. His head was brought in on a platter and given to the girl, who carried it to her mother." (Matthew 14:3-11)

Through the years, several people have asked why God did not rescue John the Baptist from prison like He rescued Peter. (Remember, an angel came and released Peter from chains while his guards slept. Acts 12) Why did God allow the wicked Herodias and the even more detestable Herod to kill one of the greatest prophets? The best answer I can offer is this: When Israel apparently would not accept Jesus as the Messiah and it became impossible for Jesus to establish His kingdom on Earth, the Father allowed John the Baptist to be killed, rather than suffer the humiliation and ridicule of being called a false prophet. If John the Baptist had lived to be as old as Methuselah (969 years), the things he predicted at the Jordan River would not have happened. This is year 2002 and still these events have not occurred, nor will they ever come to pass! The provisions given under "Plan A" are dead. John was not a false prophet. The truth he preached was conditional. Israel rejected "Plan A" and God abandoned them. The good news is that "Plan B" is unconditional. All that God has said will happen *at the appointed time.* (Revelation 9:15 shows one example of this.) The Second Coming and the establishment of God's kingdom ("Plan B") are not dependant upon human cooperation.

During the Great Tribulation, the 144,000 will accomplish their mission. **"And this gospel of the kingdom will be preached in the whole world as a testimony to all nations, and then the end will come."** (Matthew 24:14) The gospel will be preached to everyone before the end of the world comes, but most of the 144,000 will perish for speaking God's truth before the Second Coming occurs! (Revelation 11:7) John the Baptist was murdered for condemning sin, Jesus was murdered for condemning sin, and the 144,000 will suffer the same fate. Is the servant greater than the Master? Understand the powers of good and evil: Those who love sin hate the truth, and they will do everything they can to eliminate the condemnation of sin *except to repent*! People who love truth will do everything they can to remain loyal to it, even if allegiance brings death. Jesus warned, **"Everyone who does evil hates the light, and will not come into the light for fear that his deeds will be exposed. But whoever lives by the truth comes into the light, so that it may be seen plainly that what he has done has been done through God."** (John 3:20,21)

The Highest Authority

There is one last point in this study that I would like you to consider. When Jesus stood before Pilate, He gave a powerful revelation to Pilate. Consider these words, **"Once more Pilate came out and said to the Jews, 'Look, I am bringing him out to you to let you know that I find no basis for a charge against him.' When Jesus came out wearing the crown of thorns and the purple robe, Pilate said to them, 'Here is the man!' As soon as the chief priests and their officials saw him, they shouted, 'Crucify! Crucify!' But Pilate answered, 'You take him and crucify him. As for me, I find no basis for a charge against him.' The Jews insisted, 'We have a law, and according to that law he must die, because he claimed to be the Son of God.' When Pilate heard this, he was even more afraid, and he went back inside the palace. 'Where do you come from?' he asked Jesus, but Jesus gave him no answer. 'Do you refuse to speak to me?' Pilate said. 'Don't you realize I have power either to free you or to crucify you?' Jesus answered, 'You would have no power over me if it were not given to you from above. Therefore the one who handed me over to you is guilty of a greater sin."** (John 19:4-11)

Reread the words of Jesus in the last two sentences again.
Jesus told Pilate something very shocking. The Father handed
Jesus over to Pilate; otherwise, Pilate would have had no power
over Him! This principle reveals that God is intimately involved in the affairs on Earth. From this statement, I conclude
the Father also handed John the Baptist over to Herod. I am
not endorsing fatalism – "what will be – will be." Rather, I am
saying that when a person surrenders his or her will to God – as
John and Jesus did – God uses that person to accomplish His
intricate purposes. When that purpose is complete, God often
allows His loyal soldiers to rest in death until the day comes for
life eternal. I am highlighting this point because the Great
Tribulation is soon to begin and God's people have nothing to
fear as long as they submit to the higher authority of the King
of kings. Revelation says, **"If anyone is to go into captivity,
into captivity he will go. If anyone is to be killed with the
sword, with the sword he will be killed. *This calls for
patient endurance and faithfulness on the part of the
saints.*"** (Revelation 13:10, italics mine) God has a plan for His
saints. He already knows where we will end up. The question
before each of us is this: "Are we willing to allow God to use us
so that He can fulfill the purpose for which we were born?"

Jesus also told Pilate, **"Therefore, the one who handed me
over to you is guilty of a greater sin."** Jesus was speaking
about Lucifer and his demons who were present in Pilate's
judgment hall. Ultimately, Lucifer and his unseen demons
instigated the mob to hand Jesus over to Pilate. The Jews
rejected Messiah and they handed Jesus over for destruction.
Later, their punishment was total destruction in A.D. 70. Lucifer has been and still remains the instigator of hatred against
Christ from the beginning. Lucifer is the original Antichrist.
Lucifer is the father of sin and Lucifer will bear his guilt. At
the appointed time, Lucifer and his demons will provide full
restitution for their deeds. God will see to it.

144,000 Streets of Gold?

Ultimately, John the Baptist and Jesus met the same fate. God
did not establish His kingdom in John's day. These cousins died

for the same reason: They spoke the truth and the world could not bear to hear it. Is it any different today? No. When the 144,000 appear and begin to proclaim God's truth, the results will be the same. The 144,000 will be harassed and tortured and most, if not all, will perish as a result of their ministry. Nevertheless, the story does not stop there. God will resurrect and reward every one of them like Elijah! The Bible says the 144,000 will wear the names of the Father and the Son on their foreheads. (Revelation 14:1; 22:4) They will be Jesus' personal attendants in God's kingdom. The Bible says the New Jerusalem has twelve gates named after the twelve tribes of Israel, and the city's twelve foundations are named after the twelve disciples of Jesus. I just wonder if the holy city has 144,000 streets of gold – each bearing the name of God's loyal servants. Wouldn't it be wonderful if those who received salvation during the Great Tribulation lived on the street named after the servant of God who invited them to receive Jesus?

Jesus said, **"Among those born of women there has not risen anyone greater than John the Baptist; yet he who is least in the kingdom of heaven is greater than he."** This brings our study to a close. John the Baptist was not the greatest prophet to live on Earth because of who he was. John the Baptist was the greatest prophet because he preached the greatest message ever told. If announcing the first advent was the highest honor that God could bestow upon one person, what honor will be given to those who stand firm against the same rejection to herald the second and more glorious coming of Jesus?

Chapter 8

Pilate's Judgment

Jesus was born about 4 B.C. You may remember that after the wise men announced the birth of Jesus to King Herod I, the king ordered that all baby boys in Bethlehem, who were two years of age or less, should be destroyed. Ironically, Herod himself died shortly after issuing this malicious decree. Augustus Caesar honored Herod's will that stated that his kingdom was to be divided between his three surviving sons. The will gave Antipas a quarter of the realm, (the territory around Galilee), Philip a quarter of the realm (the area around Traconitis and later, Ituraea), and Archelaus the remaining half of the realm (Judea and Samaria). Each son that governed a quarter of the realm was called a "tetarch" (or a ruler of a fourth, see Luke 3:1), and Archelaus was called an "ethnarch" (a ruler of a province).

With the passage of time, Augustus did not think Archelaus was fit to be a king, so he removed Archelaus from his throne about ten years later. Archelaus was exiled and the province of Judea became a third-world Roman province that governors ruled. From A.D. 6 to the Jewish revolt in A.D. 66, governors that came from Rome's middle class ruled Judea. (The exception to this was the brief reign of Herod Agrippa I. (A.D. 41-44))

The first duty of a Roman governor was to maintain order and keep the peace according to the provisions of Roman law. Governors typically had a contingency of Roman soldiers at their command and they used them when necessary to keep order. Governors were also responsible for imposing and collecting taxes for Caesar – which was no small task given the intense animosity between the occupied territories and the heavy hand of Rome.

Then as now, people who had political ambitions coveted the office of governor, and yet, with all its trappings, the office was not very glamorous. A Roman governor walked a very fine line. He was trapped between keeping peace in a province who hated to pay taxes to Rome, while simultaneously, meeting all of Caesar's demands. If the governor offended the people, it often caused an uprising. When this occurred, Caesar would hear about it and question the governor's ability to keep the peace. If the governor tried to please the people by softening Rome's demands, Caesar would fire him in a heart beat and put him to death for insubordination. So, to be a governor in Jesus' day may have been a powerful job, but it required a delicate political balance.

Pontius Pilate

History says that Pilate was the fifth governor of Judea. Most governors served two to four years, but Pilate served as governor of Judea for about eleven years. (A.D. 26-36) We have no information about Pilate before he arrived in Judea as governor. If it were not for a few hours with Jesus on one fateful morning, Pilate would have disappeared long ago into the silent hallway of history. Josephus indicates that Pilate's career in Judea ended abruptly when he agitated his subjects one time too many. (Antiquities 18:85-89)

As the story goes, a messianic figure rose in Samaria and formed a group of enthusiastic followers. Problems became serious when they armed themselves in an attempt to deliver their people from the hands of the Romans and establish God's kingdom. To prove his assumed identity as the Messiah, the messianic figure invited his followers to follow him to the summit of Mt. Gerizim, a mountain the Samaritans considered a holy site. (See Deuteronomy 11:29.) He claimed that Moses had buried sacred vessels on top of the mountain and he knew where they were. (Evidently he believed if the sacred vessels were revealed, it would legitimize his messianic claims.) Pilate learned of this development and sent a platoon of Roman soldiers to block their ascent up the mountain. This led to a bloody confrontation and the Romans killed several Samaritans in the melee that followed. The Samaritan Council formally complained to Caesar about Pilate's abusive use of power and Tiberius summoned Pilate to Rome. Pilate left for Rome, but reached the city after Tiberius had died. The new emperor, Gaius, did not send Pilate back to Judea and Pilate suddenly disappeared from the radar screen of history.

Eusebius, a spiritual counselor to Emperor Constantine in the fourth century A.D., supports a legend that Pilate committed suicide during the reign of Gaius. The legend maintains that Pilate committed suicide due to his remorse for what he did to Jesus. (Hist. Eccl. 2.7.1) History does not reveal if Pilate became a born-again Christian. However, it is interesting that Christian churches in northern Africa years later declared Pilate a saint. In fact, Tertullian claims that Pilate was a Christian at heart in a letter he wrote to Tiberius. (Apology 21) I believe that Pilate had a complete change of heart after meeting Jesus, and his actions in the drama you are about to read are quite revealing, when put in context.

Even though we do not actually know what happened to Pilate in the end, we do know what happened on Friday morning, April 7, A.D. 30, when a long sequence of events brought an unsuspecting Pilate face to face with God. All four gospels record descriptions of this unrehearsed confrontation. This will be the focus of this chapter because there are profound end time parallels between the events that transpired in Pilate's judgment hall and events that will happen in courtrooms all over the world during the Great Tribulation.

Note: To review Pilate's experience, I have taken excerpts from the gospels and attempted to put them in chronological order. You may note some redundancy since each gospel describes the events with a slightly different perspective. It is my hope that this study will reveal something about Pilate that you may not have noticed before. Insertions in brackets [ ] and italics are mine and are added for clarity or emphasis.

John Begins the Story

"Then the Jews led Jesus from Caiaphas [the High Priest] to the palace of the Roman governor [Pilate]. By now it was early morning, and to avoid ceremonial uncleanness the Jews did not enter the palace; they wanted to be able to eat the Passover. So Pilate came out [of his palace] to them and asked, 'What charges are you bringing against this man?' 'If he were not a criminal,' they replied, 'we would not have handed him over to you.' Pilate said, 'Take him yourselves and judge him by your own law.' 'But we have no right to execute anyone,' the Jews objected. This [response] happened so that the words Jesus had spoken [Luke 18:31-33] indicating the kind of death he was going to die would be fulfilled.

Pilate then went back inside the palace, [he] summoned Jesus and asked him, 'Are you the king of the Jews?' 'Is that your own idea,' Jesus asked, 'or did others talk to you about me?' 'Am I a Jew [that I should care]?' Pilate replied. 'It was *your* people and *your* chief priests who handed you over to me. What is it you have done?' Jesus said, 'My kingdom is not of this world. If it were, my servants would fight to prevent my arrest by the Jews. But now my kingdom is from another place.' '[So!] You are a king, then!' said Pilate. Jesus answered, 'You are right in saying I am a king. In fact, for this reason I was born, and for this I came into the world, to testify to the truth. *Everyone on the side of truth listens to me.*' 'What is truth?' [a puzzled] Pilate asked. With this he went out again to the Jews and said, 'I find no basis for a charge against him.' " (John 18:28-38)

Commentary:

Pilate's fairness is seen in his first report to the Jews. Pilate knew of Jesus' reputation. He had heard of His miracles and in a secular way, he quickly decided that Jesus was not a common criminal or rabble rouser. Pilate did not have a religious heart, therefore the teachings of Jesus, which infuriated the Jews, did not personally offend him. After listening to Jesus for a few moments, Pilate sensed the Jewish leaders and Jesus were embroiled in a religious squabble "over words" and he really did not want to get involved. Pilate returned to the waiting crowd and *boldly declared Jesus to be innocent.*

Luke Says

"But they insisted, 'He stirs up the people all over Judea by his teaching. He started in Galilee and has come all the way here.' On hearing this, Pilate asked if the man was a Galilean. When he learned that Jesus was under Herod's jurisdiction [Herod Antipas]**, he** [Pilate conveniently recused himself on this civil matter and] **sent him to Herod, who was also in Jerusalem at that time** [to observe Passover]**."**

Commentary:

Pilate and Herod Antipas had a long history as political enemies and in the quicksand of this situation, Pilate saw a golden opportunity. By sending Jesus to Antipas, Pilate flattered the king's ego by showing respect, but Pilate also had a political motive. He was trying to escape further confrontation with his contentious subjects, the Jews.

"When Herod saw Jesus, he was greatly pleased, because for a long time he had been wanting to see him. From what he had heard about him, he hoped to see him perform some miracle. He plied him with many questions, but Jesus gave him no answer. The chief priests and the teachers of the law were standing there, vehemently accusing him. Then Herod and his soldiers ridiculed and mocked him. Dressing him in an elegant robe, they sent him back to Pilate [because Antipas did not want to offend the high priest and because of possible political repercussions, Herod made sure Jesus was Pilate's problem]**. That day Herod and Pilate became friends – before this they had been enemies."**

"[A couple hours later] **Pilate called together the chief priests, the rulers and the people, and said to them, 'You brought me this man as one who was inciting the people to rebellion. I have examined him in your presence and have found no basis for your charges against him. Neither has Herod, for he sent him back to us; as you can see, he has done nothing to deserve death. Therefore,** [in an effort to please you, how about this?] **I will punish him** [for stirring up trouble] **and then release him.' "** (Luke 23:5-16)

Commentary:

Pilate declared Jesus was innocent a second time.

Matthew Says

Now it was the governor's custom at the [Passover] **Feast to** [gain the favor of the Jews and] **release a prisoner chosen by the crowd. At that time they had a notorious prisoner, called** [Jesus Barabbas or just] **Barabbas. So when the crowd had gathered** [at his palace]**, Pilate** [sought to set Jesus free through negotiation. So he] **asked them, 'Which one do you want me to release to you:** [Jesus who is called] **Barabbas, or Jesus who is called Christ?' For** [now] **he knew it was out of envy that they had handed Jesus over to him."**

Commentary:

At this point, Pilate was convinced that Jesus was innocent of all the charges that the Jewish leaders had brought against Him. So, Pilate attempted to reason with them, comparing the worst of society (Barabbas) with the best (Jesus). The hostility directed toward this innocent man amazed Pilate. I believe he sensed there was something supernatural about the intensity of the clamor.

"While Pilate was sitting on the judge's seat, his wife sent him this message: 'Don't have anything to do with that innocent man, for I have suffered a great deal today in a dream because of him.' But the chief priests

and the elders persuaded the crowd to ask for Barabbas and to have Jesus executed. 'Which of the two do you want me to release to you?' asked the governor. 'Barabbas,' they answered. 'What shall I do, then, with Jesus who is called Christ?' Pilate asked. They all answered, 'Crucify him!' 'Why? What crime has he committed?' asked Pilate. But they shouted all the louder, 'Crucify him!' "

Commentary:

The note Pilate received from his wife stunned him. After reading her comments, the truth planted in his mind by the Holy Spirit was confirmed. This was no ordinary trial. Jesus *was* the Son of God, the predicted Messiah. At that moment, the tables turned. Pilate suddenly found himself on trial. What should he do with Jesus? Pilate had the power to set Jesus free and he had the power to crucify Him. If Pilate set Jesus free, the mob would go crazy and Caesar would question his ability to govern. If he crucified Jesus, Pilate knew an innocent man, even the Messiah, would be put to death. Pilate had to make a choice! In exasperation, Pilate uttered a sentence that every sinner who comes under the convicting power of the Holy Spirit has had to ask: "What shall I do then, with Jesus, who is called Christ?" The mob's reaction became unreasonable. Pilate raised his voice above the noise of the crowd asking, "What crime has He committed?" The response was deafening. Pilate discovered an awful truth: There is no reason in rebellion.

"When Pilate saw that he was getting nowhere [and he had no political options left], but that instead an uproar was starting, he took water and washed his hands in front of the crowd. 'I am innocent of this man's blood,' he said. 'It is your responsibility!' All the people answered, 'Let his blood be on us and on our children!' Then he released Barabbas to them. But he had Jesus flogged, and [after further discussion with the Jews, Pilate] handed him over to be crucified." (Matthew 27:15-26)

Commentary:

When the week began, Pilate had no idea what would occur on Friday morning. Suddenly, God powerfully catapulted Pilate to the forefront of an incredible moment of truth and he, the governor of Judea, like the apostle Peter a few hours earlier, proved to be a coward. Pilate had a lot at stake. In order to keep his prestigious job as governor, he had to demonstrate skills worthy of his appointment. In order to satisfy the protests of angry Jews, he had to offer them something. Pilate was convicted that Jesus was innocent, yet he sought to deflect his guilt by simply washing his hands of this murderous event. Consider the irony of his action. The Jews who were standing before Pilate, believed that they had to be ceremonially clean for the Passover. To maintain their "cleanliness," they would not allow themselves to enter Pilate's palace, yet within their own hearts they harbored such hatred and malice toward Jesus, they were willing to murder Him. Neither the Jews' sanctimonious ceremonies nor the water used by Pilate could remove the stain of sin. The only thing in the whole universe that can wash away the guilt of sin is the sinless blood of Jesus.

Both Peter and Pilate discovered something about themselves that day. The apostle Peter discovered the cowardice within his own character when he denied knowing Jesus, just as Pilate also discovered his cowardly character when he allowed an innocent man to be put to death. Pilate thought that if he had Jesus flogged (a punishment of indescribable agony), the Jews would relent and their rage would be satisfied – in which case, Pilate could save Jesus from death.

John Says

"Then Pilate took Jesus and had him flogged. The soldiers twisted together a crown of thorns and put it on his head. They clothed him in a purple robe and went up to him again, saying, 'Hail, king of the Jews!' And they struck him in the face."

Commentary:

After the blows and the flogging, I am sure Jesus was barely conscious. He had received the harshest treatment possible this side of death.

"Once more Pilate came out and said to the Jews, 'Look, I am bringing him out to you to let you know that I find no basis for a charge against him.' When Jesus came out wearing the crown of thorns and the purple robe, Pilate said to them, 'Here is the man!' As soon as the chief priests and their officials saw him, they shouted, 'Crucify! Crucify!' But Pilate answered, 'You take him and crucify him. As for me, I find no basis for a charge against him.' The Jews insisted, 'We have a law, and according to that law he must die, because he claimed to be the Son of God.' When Pilate heard this, he was even more afraid, and he went back inside the palace [to speak with Jesus]."

Commentary:

Every human heart is capable of feeling the hatred the Jews expressed toward Jesus that morning. It only takes the right circumstances and issues to align. Pilate was trapped in a power play between Heaven and Hell. I believe that every demon possible, who had formerly enjoyed the glories of Heaven, was present to ensure that their Creator was destroyed. Lucifer, the Antichrist himself, was present – using every influence and every power in his arsenal to torture and destroy his holy Adversary. A watching universe shuddered to see the depths that sin-full hearts can sink. Pilate knew in his own way that Jesus was the Messiah and when the Jews said, "He claimed to be the Son of God," they ironically confirmed a truth that had previously stirred the heart of the governor. At that moment, he became "even more afraid."

During the Great Tribulation, circumstances and issues will align in such a way that everyone on Earth will be forced into a situation like Pilate faced – not to judge Jesus, but to be judged by Jesus. **"For we must all appear before the judgment**

seat of Christ, that each one may receive what is due him for the things done while in the body, whether good or bad." (2 Corinthians 5:10) The Holy Spirit allowed Pilate to know the truth about Jesus. His wife's note was not a coincidence, but instead it was a message from Heaven. *In desperation Pilate declared Christ's innocence a third time, yet he could not bring himself to set Jesus free and face the ridicule for doing the right thing.* This is a parallel of how it will be during the Great Tribulation. The will of God will be set before the world in terms that are as bright as the noonday Sun, yet few will have the strength of character to stand up and take the ridicule for doing God's will. No wonder Revelation says, **"But the *cowardly*, the unbelieving, the vile, the murderers, the sexually immoral, those who practice magic arts, the idolaters and all liars – their place will be in the fiery lake of burning sulfur. This is the second death."** (Revelation 21:8) Let us be real. Every human being is a coward and will not take a stand for truth unless they are infused with Holy Spirit power, which can help them stand courageously through trials of faith.

"[A troubled Pilate interviewed Jesus again.] 'Where do you come from?' he asked Jesus, but Jesus gave him no answer. 'Do you refuse to speak to me?' Pilate said. 'Don't you realize I have power either to free you or to crucify you?' Jesus answered, 'You would have no power over me if it were not given to you from above. Therefore the one who handed me over to you is guilty of a greater sin.' "

Commentary:

Pilate condemned himself with his own words when he told Jesus that he had the power to set Him free. Jesus, knowing that He had come into the world to set us "free," did not address Pilate's cowardice. Instead, Jesus condemned Lucifer, who truly was responsible and guilty for handing Jesus over to be killed. When the demons heard these words, I believe they shuddered. The mouth of God declared that He would annihi-

late Lucifer. Meanwhile, Pilate's consternation was on a
different plane. For the first time, Pilate recognized a fatal
flaw in his own character. He could not bring himself to do the
right thing. Pilate knew Jesus was innocent and believed
Jesus was the Son of God, the Messiah. He also knew that
Jesus was hated *for no other reason than declaring who He
was.* Jesus was the King of kings!

**"From then on, Pilate tried to set Jesus free, but the
Jews kept shouting, 'If you let this man go, you are no
friend of Caesar. Anyone who claims to be a king opposes Caesar.' When Pilate heard this, he brought Jesus
out and sat down on the judge's seat at a place known as
the Stone Pavement (which in Aramaic is Gabbatha). It
was the day of Preparation of Passover Week, about the
sixth hour** [noon]. [When the audience became silent, Pilate
spoke soberly from a deep spiritual awakening within.] **'Here
is your king,' Pilate said to the Jews. But they shouted,
'Take him away! Take him away! Crucify him!' 'Shall I
crucify *your* king?' Pilate asked. 'We have no king but
Caesar,' the chief priests answered. Finally Pilate
handed him over to them to be crucified. So the soldiers took charge of Jesus."** (John 19:1-16)

Commentary:

Believing that Jesus was the Son of God was not enough to
stop Pilate from acquiescing to the demands of the Jews.
Simply knowing the truth will not prevent you from denying
the truth. Peter and Pilate represent both sides of this dilemma. Even though Peter was religious and personally knew
Jesus, he still denied him. On the other hand, Pilate was
secular, but he knew Jesus was innocent and still sent Him to
His death.

In an effort to mitigate his guilt and show some support for
Jesus, Pilate did the following:

"Pilate [deliberately] **had a notice prepared and fastened
to the cross. It read: JESUS OF NAZARETH, THE KING
OF THE JEWS. Many of the Jews read this sign, for the**

place where Jesus was crucified was near the city, and the sign was written in Aramaic, Latin and Greek. The chief priests of the Jews protested to Pilate, 'Do not write "The King of the Jews," but that this man claimed to be king of the Jews.' Pilate answered, 'What I have written, I have written [and it will remain unchanged because I believe him].' " (John 19:19-22)

"Joseph of Arimathea, a prominent member of the Council, who was himself waiting for the kingdom of God, went boldly to Pilate and asked for Jesus' body. Pilate was surprised to hear that he was already dead [since death by crucifixion usually took days]. Summoning the centurion, he asked him if Jesus had already died. When he learned from the centurion that it was so, he gave the body to Joseph." (Mark 15:43-45)

"The next day [Saturday], the one after Preparation Day, the chief priests and the Pharisees went to Pilate. 'Sir,' they said, 'we remember that while he was still alive that deceiver said, "After three days I will rise again." So give the order for the tomb to be made secure until the third day. Otherwise, his disciples may come and steal the body and tell the people that he has been raised from the dead. This last deception will be worse than the first.' 'Take a guard,' Pilate answered. 'Go, make the tomb as secure as you know how.' So they went and made the tomb secure by putting a seal on the stone and posting the guard." (Matthew 27:62-66)

Commentary:

The Bible does not indicate if Pilate knew about the predicted resurrection of Jesus. Sensing the Jews' desire to cover their deed and keep the peace, Pilate may have cooperated with them. Even better, if Pilate was aware that a resurrection might be possible, *his* guards could validate the event for him if they were present.

"[On Sunday morning] While the women were on their way [to tell the disciples about the empty tomb], some of the guards went into the city and reported to the chief priests everything that had happened. When the chief priests had met with the elders and devised a plan, they gave the soldiers a large sum of money, telling them, 'You are to say, "His disciples came during the night and stole him away while we were asleep." If this report gets to [Pilate] the governor, we will satisfy him and keep you out of trouble.' So the soldiers took the money and did as they were instructed. And this [false] story has been widely circulated among the Jews to this very day." (Matthew 28:11-15)

Commentary:

Pilate awoke on that Friday morning only to discover it was *his* day of judgment. Yes, Pilate sat in the judgment seat, but Pilate was on trial. Pilate declared Jesus was innocent three times. Still, Pilate had Jesus flogged and crucified rather than take any ridicule from the Jews and a possible reprimand from Caesar. When that day ended, I am sure that Pilate was not the same. You cannot violate your innermost sense of fairness and justice, and still have respect for yourself. Pilate violated "the right" to keep his job. Peter violated "his loyalty" to keep his dignity. Both men lost the very thing they sought to protect.

Conclusions:

Given the scant history we have about Pilate, I would like to offer the following scenario about the end of Pilate's life. When the guards reported to Pilate their personal experience at the tomb on Sunday morning, inwardly Pilate was overjoyed. Imagine that! Jesus really is the Son of God! When Pilate put the details of Christ's birth, life and death together, he became a silent believer in Jesus. When Pilate sent his soldiers to intercept the "messianic figure" from Samaria six years later, he gave orders to destroy the movement because it was an insult to Jesus, who according to reliable sources, had ascended into Heaven. The "uncalled for brutality" of Pilate's soldiers aroused the Samaritan Council, who appealed to

Tiberius Caesar. He summoned Pilate to Rome for a reprimand. Tiberius died before Pilate arrived in Rome and his
successor, Gaius, relieved Pilate of his career. Pilate eventually settled in northern Africa where he confessed to being a
believer in Christ. He found refuge in Alexandria among the
Christians who had also found refuge from Rome's hatred
there. (This may explain why the Coptic and Ethiopian
churches later made him a saint.) In time, Pilate became ill
and impoverished. I am sure he often relived that infamous
day and probably never forgave himself for having Jesus
flogged and crucified. In a depressed and lonely state of mind,
he may have ended his life. Ironically, legend says that when
Peter eventually faced his own death on a cross, he asked to be
crucified upside down, since he was not worthy to die as Christ
had died. Evidently, both men died without being able to
forgive themselves of their cowardice. However, the good news
of the gospel is that Jesus forgave them both, and because of
their faith in Christ as the Lamb of God, I sincerely hope to
see *both* men in Heaven.

Chapter 9

Noah and the Pig Pen

Most Christians already know there is an end time parallel between Noah's day and the end of the world. Remember, Jesus said, **"As it was in the days of Noah, so it will be at the coming of the Son of Man. For in the days before the flood, people were eating and drinking, marrying and giving in marriage, up to the day Noah entered the ark; and they knew nothing about what would happen until the flood came and took them all away. That is how it will be at the coming of the Son of Man."** (Matthew 24:36-38) These words are a bit of a mystery. What did Jesus mean when He said, **"and they knew nothing about what would happen until the flood came and took them all away"**? Peter says Noah was a *preacher* of righteousness. (2 Peter 2:5) If Noah was a preacher of righteousness, then it seems fair to conclude that the antidiluvians were warned for 120 years. How could the antediluvians not have known about what Noah did and said? Think about it! Noah built the most unusual object of his time: a huge boat! Even more incredible, God mysteriously marched the animals into the ark just days before it rained. It seems inconceivable that the antediluvians did not know anything about what would happen after seeing all of this. How could they have missed the warning message and basically ignored the physical evidence that a flood was coming? I have a possible answer, but I will withhold it for a moment. Let there be no mistake. God did not put the story of Noah in the Bible to entertain us. Jesus warned that Noah's experience will be paralleled at the end of the world. The events of Noah's day had dreadful consequences and so will ours.

The Days of Noah

"Now the Earth was corrupt in God's sight and was full of violence. God saw how corrupt the Earth had become, for

all the people on Earth had corrupted their ways. . . . The Lord saw how great man's wickedness on the Earth had become, and that every inclination of the thoughts of his heart was only evil all the time. The Lord was grieved that he had made man on the Earth, and his heart was filled with pain. So the Lord said, 'I will wipe mankind, whom I have created, from the face of the Earth – men and animals, and creatures that move along the ground, and birds of the air – for I am grieved that I have made them.' But Noah found favor in the eyes of the Lord." (Genesis 6:11,12,5-8, italics mine)

According to the Bible, there are 1,656 years between the time when Adam and Eve were created and when the Earth was destroyed by a flood. This may sound like a long time, but do not forget, men lived much longer then. Today, it is hard to imagine that the lives of *two* men, Adam and his sixth generation grandson Methuselah, extended through most of this period. In fact, Grandpa Adam lived 243 years *after* Methuselah was born, so he was very well acquainted with Methuselah. Methuselah died on or about the year of the flood. The horrible state of degeneracy achieved by the antediluvians in 1,656 years demonstrates a very interesting point about fallen man. If God had not dramatically reduced the life span of the human race after the flood, He would have had to destroy the world *several times* during the past 4,500 years. Reducing the length of life has dramatically reduced the amount of evil one generation can perpetuate.

When you ponder God's long suffering, compassion and love and all that He gave to redeem humanity at Calvary, considering that God *justifiably* destroyed the world in Noah's day is an awesome thing. God's deliberate destruction of Earth proves three things. First, God *closely* observes this planet and its inhabitants. Second, when sin exceeds the threshold of God's wisdom and patience, there is *no* recovery. Third, man's degenerate behavior *always* matures to a point where total destruction is the best solution. These three facts also explain the rise and fall of 21 civilizations on Earth. God raises a nation of people, and when their behavior reaches the threshold of God's patience, they are destroyed. Wake up America (and every other nation)!

It is amazing that many people, even Christians, deny that God was responsible for the flood in Noah's day. They cannot believe that a God of love would deliberately drown men, women and children and wipe the Earth clean of life! Calvary and other events recorded in the Bible prove that God is love, but His love is poorly understood. God's wisdom is infinite and allows Him to see far into the future. He destroys corrupt and evil nations for the benefit of nations that are yet to come! What would this world be like today if God had not destroyed the antediluvians some 4,500 years ago? The claim, "God does not kill," is a rebellious distortion of God's justice and mercy. Consider His testimony: **"So the Lord said, 'I will wipe mankind, whom I have created, from the face of the Earth – men and animals, and creatures that move along the ground, and birds of the air – for I am grieved that I have made them.' "** Also, notice this statement: **". . . I am the Lord, and there is no other. I form the light and create darkness, I bring prosperity and create disaster; I, the Lord, do all these things."** (Isaiah 45:6,7)

When people claim that God does not destroy people, we have a perfect example of the same inebriated theology that existed before the flood. God has not changed. He is the same eternal God yesterday, today, and tomorrow. God has always been merciful and just. He is patient and longsuffering. He generously extends mercy to sinners *until* extended mercy fails to produce a redemptive effect. When it becomes impossible to redeem sinners, God's wrath against sin is unrestrained and He cauterizes the malignancy of sin by destroying those who refuse to love righteousness. Look at the sordid history of Israel in the Old Testament. God's actions with Israel are a mirror of how He has dealt with all nations from the beginning of time.

Moral Novocaine

God's actions in Noah's day proves that sin is a one-way street to destruction. Our world is becoming like Noah's day once again because sin works like a shot of Novocaine. It deadens our thinking, clouds and distorts our feelings, and colors our understanding of right and wrong. When sin stupefies the reasoning powers of a person, base passions become dominate. When base passions rule, people commit horrible deeds to satisfy uncontrollable lust or obsession. Day after day, newspapers confirm that we live in an age when carnal passions rule, and it seems that many people are unable to reason. Sin, like its twin sister, the grave, is relentless in its quest – steadily tightening its control over the nations and, ultimately, the world.

Although the first six chapters of the Bible do not give us many details about Noah's situation, we can consider the sinful world today and compare it with what behavior must have been like in Noah's day. *It is an end time parallel in reverse:* Jesus said, **"Now the Earth was corrupt in God's sight and was full of violence. . . . for all the people on earth had corrupted their ways. . . . people were eating and drinking, marrying and giving in marriage, up to the day Noah entered the ark. . . ."** These verses are full of meaning when viewed in the backdrop of Noah's day. Remember that Noah preached his heart out for 120 years and the antediluvians **"knew nothing about what would happen until the flood came and took them all away."** We have to wonder, "How can this be?" The answer is moral Novocaine. At first, Noah's preaching was a spectacle, an oddity, a news item, a folly. It did not take long before Noah's peers regarded him as a kook, a doomsayer, a pest, a cult leader and a nuisance. After a few years of sounding like a broken record, no one listened to Noah because the antediluvians had become intoxicated with sin. They became consumed with debasing entertainment, debauchery, sexual immorality, gluttony, greed and the pursuit of every sensual pleasure. They lived without concern for tomorrow – eating and drinking, giving parties (marriage feasts), etc. The antediluvians lived for hundreds of years and they would not believe Noah's message: Time was limited, and the time for the age of the antediluvians was about to end! Centuries passed and they were lulled into believing there was an endless supply of time. I do not want to sound like I am saying that life for everyone was pleasant in Noah's day. Corruption brings violence, murder, physical and emotional abuse for children, cheating, lying, stealing, sexual immorality, hatred and strife. Sin has two faces (two-faced). One side may be comedy, but the other is tragedy. In fact, it is the tragic side of sin that motivates sinners toward comedy. The truth is that there is no genuine happiness in sin and there is no peace and satisfaction in wrong doing. There may be shallow moments of laughter and hilarity, because sin offers pleasure for a short season. However, sin's comedy and its pleasures are as fleeting as darkness at sunrise. When a person commits a sin, God sends the gift of guilt so that repentance and reformation can occur. Unfortunately, moral Novocaine numbs this gift of guilt. The antediluvians never realized how offensive they were in God's sight.

Jesus said, **"They knew nothing about what would happen until the flood came and took them all away"** because Jesus Himself was present during the flood. Jesus walked and talked with Noah and commanded him to build the ark. Jesus, the Creator of Earth, sent the flood! As Jesus looked forward to our day, He gave us the warning parallel **"as it was in the days of Noah. . . ."**

Odd-ball Noah

The Bible says, **"But Noah found favor in the eyes of the Lord."** (Genesis 6:8) Why did Jesus look favorably on Noah? Why did Jesus select Noah to build an ark? **"This is the account of Noah. Noah was a righteous man, blameless among the people of his time, and he walked with God."** (Genesis 6:9) Noah was a genius. We know this because Noah feared the Lord and the Bible says "the fear the Lord" is the first thing a smart person discovers! (Psalm 111:10) I believe that Noah was considered an odd-ball in his community because he walked with God. Noah did not participate in the decadent and indulgent behavior of his time. I am sure he was not popular or well liked because God's people are always out of step with the ways of the world. Jesus told His disciples: **"If you belonged to the world, it would love you as its own. As it is, you do not belong to the world, but I have chosen you out of the world. That is why the world hates you."** (John 15:19) Light and darkness can never walk together and be compatible.

In my mind's eye, I see Noah and the Lord walking together constantly. In one of these walks, the Lord told Noah that He was going to destroy the Earth. Jesus explained to Noah that He had no option but to cauterize the malignant growth of sin by cleansing the world with a great flood of water. (The next cleansing will be with fire.) The Lord explained to Noah that the survival of animal, plant and human life depended on Noah building a great boat. I assume that Noah was wealthy, for he must have borne the costs of building the ark. No doubt, Noah was a very knowledgeable man in areas such as engineering, biology, personnel and project management, animal husbandry, botany, nutrition and other sciences. Even so, given the daunting size of the task, Noah must have been overwhelmed. Although Noah was in the prime of life at 480 years of age when the Lord commanded him to cut the first tree, some of the issues that he may have had to address were:

1. Noah had to methodically exchange or convert his possessions to currency, in order to meet payroll and material purchases.

2. To save as many people as possible, Noah had to give frequent seminars warning the people about the coming flood and the end of life as they knew it. After a while, fewer and fewer people attended, until eventually, no one showed up.

3. I can imagine that Noah hired people to collect and preserve thousands of various kinds of seeds. These would have to be gathered, sorted and cataloged for regeneration after the flood. Containers and food for thousands of insects had to be constructed and arranged. Noah was responsible for gathering samples of every living thing and placing them aboard the ark so that they might survive the flood.

4. Noah hired hundreds of people to cut and transport trees. At the building site, Noah's employees shaped and assembled the trees according to the plans which the Lord had given him. Noah spent many years working with the employees making sure the great boat was built according to divine specifications.

Building the ark was hard work. There was much to do, much to learn and no time to waste. Think about it. All the life that God had created (minus the fish) were reduced to a few thousand samples stored in a wooden boat for about a year. God made the world in six days, but it took Noah and his employees 120 years to gather the sufficient varieties necessary to replenish the world after the flood.

Noah's Family

Noah had a very supportive family. Without a doubt, disposing personal property and cherished possessions was painful. However, this had to be done, because every square inch of the ark was designed for sustaining life and had very little space for personal belongings. It would be fair to say that Noah probably sold everything he owned to pay for the ark. Can you imagine how Noah's wife must have felt when their remaining possessions were sold to cover their last expenses? The good news is that the process of building the ark did not cost Noah his family.

Noah's three sons were married, but none of them had children at the time of the flood. Can you imagine what it must have been like for Noah's daughters-in-law to go to their parents and plead with them to come into the ark for the last time? I can only imagine their heart-felt anguish when their parents and siblings refused to go. Can you imagine Noah's grief when none of his employees would enter the very ark they had helped to build?

If we were to switch places with Noah within the context of our lives today, not very many people would be willing to do what Noah did. Few people in today's world have that kind of faith, character, courage and stamina to deal with the ridicule, threats, sacrifice and toil. Almost no one is up to such a challenge. What does Noah's actions say about his faith in God? As I have considered Noah, I have concluded that even if there had been no flood, Noah would have been willing to build the ark because Noah was willing to do anything that God wanted. *This was Noah's faith.*

End Time Parallels

Three things about Noah's life and experience stand out. First, **"Noah did everything just as God commanded him. The Lord then said to Noah, 'Go into the ark, you and your whole family, because I have found you righteous in this generation.' "** (Genesis 6:22, 7:1) Noah's faith produced obedience, and when the last day arrived, a compassionate God declared Noah righteous and directed him into *the ark of safety.* The end time parallel is this: During the Great Tribulation, worshiping God as He commanded, including the fourth commandment, will be a difficult test of faith. True faith in God produces obedience *at any cost.* Remember why Nebuchadnezzar threw Daniel's three friends into the fiery furnace? They were put in the furnace because they refused to worship King Nebuchadnezzar's image. (Daniel 3) During the Great Tribulation, everyone who refuses to worship the image of the beast will be threatened with death. (Revelation 13:15) The good news is that everyone who passes the worship test of faith will be declared righteous and sealed with the righteousness of Christ. This sealing will be *the ark of safety* for our day.

Second, the Bible says, **"By faith Noah, when warned about things not yet seen, in holy fear built an ark to save his family. By his faith he condemned the world and became heir of the righteousness that comes by faith."** (Hebrews 7:11) The Bible says that Noah condemned *the* world by obeying God. This means that during the Great Tribulation, some people will submit to the authority of God, and by doing this, they will prove that it can be done! If it is possible for one faith-filled person to obey God's commandments, then people who refuse to obey them will be condemned because they, too, could have obeyed. This is how Noah condemned the world. God, through Noah, invited everyone to get on the ark, but no one accepted His invitation except Noah and his family. God drowned every other living person on Earth. The same situation will exist during the Great Tribulation. Through His 144,000 servants, God will invite everyone on Earth to submit to the authority of Jesus Christ by worshiping Him. Many people will submit because of their faith in God, but the rest of humanity will be destroyed.

The last element about Noah's story that stands out concerns the seven days of waiting. **"The Lord then said to Noah, 'Go into the ark, you and your whole family, because I have found you righteous in this generation. . . . Seven days from now I will send rain on the earth for forty days and forty nights, and I will wipe from the face of the earth every living creature I have made.' And Noah did all that the Lord commanded him."** (Genesis 7:1,4,5) For seven days, the ark sat strangely silent on the hilltop where it had rested during its construction. The townspeople did not concern themselves with the silence. The local "newspaper" mocked Noah saying that he and his family were trapped in the ark with hundreds of animals. An unseen hand closed the giant door to the ark, which no man could move.

I see the gathering of the animals into the ark as very ironic. God wanted to gather people into the ark, but they would not come, so He gathered up the animals. If the antediluvians had not been so numb with sin, this extraordinary event would have caused sober reflection. Instead, it became a point of laughter and ridicule. I can hear them taunt, "So, Noah has built a zoo!" As the hours and days passed, the revelers forgot Noah and the ark as they focused on their daily routines. I believe at midnight on the seventh day, a huge bolt of lightning tore the sky from East to West and peals of deafening thunder echoed the end of mercy. Droplets of water from Heaven became torrents driven by powerful winds and the floodgates of the deep were opened producing gigantic geysers. Suddenly, water was rising rapidly everywhere. How long do you think it took for the numbness of the Novocaine of sin to wear off? Panic and fear filled every house. Noah's testimony was true! Their recognition of truth came too late – forever too late. God had sealed the giant door of the ark and even Noah could not open it to receive desperate passengers. God had spoken for 120 years and He had nothing more to say. The time had come. All the wicked people must die. God could have motivated every antediluvian into the ark through fear. If He had left a door open, they would have gotten on board. However, in God's economy, a person is not saved by fear. A person is saved by faith or not at all.

The end time parallel is identical. When the events of the seventh trumpet begin, every person alive will have made a choice – to receive the seal of God or the mark of the beast. It is at this moment that God will close the great door of mercy in Heaven. God will terminate His generous offer of salvation. The wicked cannot harm people who have God's seal. A bolt of lightning will tear the sky from East to West and peals of deafening thunder will signal "salvation is finished." Burning hailstones will rain down from the sky and the a global earthquake will rip the Earth into pieces. (Revelation 11:15-19) Within minutes, a great sign will appear in Heaven. Everyone on Earth will look up and see the Ark of the Covenant displayed in the heavens. *That ark* contains God's holy law. God will show the Ark of the Covenant to the world for the same reason He showed rain to the antediluvians. Because they refused to believe there was a holy law, the wicked will be condemned. Now that their rebellion has been exposed, the wicked will need to be destroyed. The seven last plagues will fall on them and the wicked will all be destroyed by the time the seventh plague is finished. Once again, unbelievers must perish. God has decreed it.

An Antidote for the Novocaine of Sin

If we do not make a determined effort to pray and search God's Word for greater truth *each* day, it is inevitable that we will become desensitized by sin. I remember the first time we drove through Nebraska. Shirley and I were returning from Seattle and we did not know about the big hog farms located in that state. I was driving along enjoying the open road when suddenly we encountered a overwhelming stench that took our breath away. I looked around expecting to see some big carcass beside the road. I grabbed a tissue to cover my nose. The smell was overpowering. I had been driving about 70 mph, but I sped up, hoping to escape the odor. I remember thinking to myself, "Man, I don't know what was killed, but it must have been huge to stink this much." The faster we went, the worse the smell became. After a few miles, I saw some signs and I realized the overpowering stench was not from a dead animal, but from living animals – thousands of pigs!

I was surprised their pungent odor permeated so many square miles. I remember thinking to myself, "This must be how this Earth smells to God." No wonder God required the priest to use incense in the earthly temple. I was amazed that local people did not notice the odor! I have since learned that people who live in or near the pig farms do not notice the smell of their pigs unless an unusually strong breeze puts it in their face. Sin has the same effect. The foul odor of sin often goes unnoticed by the people of this world. We have grown accustomed to it. It is the way of life in every culture. A few months after the smelly incident in Nebraska, I was conducting a seminar in Colorado and mentioned this experience to the audience. During a break in the seminar, a man came up to me and said, "I owned a large pig farm for 30 years and the odor did not bother me until we sold the farm and moved into town. I never understood why people became so aggravated by the smell of my pigs until we moved away and my own nose was cleaned out!"

When the farmer moved away from his pigs, his nose began to work! When we distance ourselves from Sodom and Gomorrah, we see how wicked sin is! Sin, like Novocaine, deadens our senses. The antediluvians did not take Noah's message seriously because they were spiritually numb. They could not comprehend their offensiveness in God's sight. The same problem exists today. The carnal mind does not realize the strength of its rebellion against God until it is directly confronted with God's will. God confronted Pharaoh with His commands and Pharaoh refused ten times! The antediluvians were confronted with God's plans for 120 years and they refused to enter the ark. During the Great Tribulation, God will confront every man, woman and child with His authority expressed in the Ten Commandments and a majority of the world will rebel. There is an antidote for the Novocaine of sin! We have a Savior from sin and He has sent the Holy Spirit to everyone – offering freedom from sin.

There is a law that says, "By beholding, we become changed." Lot's family became desensitized to Sodom's sinful ways by living in that pig pen for a few years. Unless we fill our minds with God's Word and pray for spiritual discernment each day, the stench of sin will gradually disappear and sin will become tolerable. The antidote for the Novocaine of sin is walking with God. Noah, Enoch, and Abraham walked with God! These men knew that every act of sin gives birth to sorrow, heartache and ultimately death. Sin *can be* so tempting. Sin may look like a "piece of cake" or in Eve's case, "a beautiful piece of fruit," but sin is an illusion. The devil markets sin with all the glitter and glamour the carnal mind can create, but when sin reaches maturity it is very painful to see. Who feels euphoric after visiting a ward of AIDS victims? Who gets a rush of joy after looking at a rape or murder victim? Who feels great after learning that his or her house has been broken into and the valuables stolen? It is ironic that sinners dislike the consequences of sin. We know that sin is powerful because the word "forbidden" means nothing when the passion for sin is roused. If our minds are not renewed by God's Word and ennobled by God's Spirit, sin will captivate us, numb us, deceive us and ultimately destroy us. This is why God hates sin.

When Jesus sailed across the Sea of Galilee to the region of the Gaderenes, two demoniacs who were living in or near a pig pen met Him. (Matthew 8:28-32) Jesus could see these tortured men desired to be set free, but He also saw they were powerless against the mighty demons that had conquered them. Jesus used this occasion to create a wonderful object lesson. *Freedom from the dominion of sin is only possible through Christ.* Because He loved them, Jesus set the helpless men free. He commanded the demons to leave the men and enter a large herd of pigs that were nearby. Immediately the men became joyful and sane, but the pigs became wild and disoriented and they ran into the lake and drowned themselves. An old adage goes like this: "If people do not resist the devil, they become a dwelling for the devil." Evidently, these two men had not resisted the influence of demons and many demons possessed them. Likewise, demons possessed the antediluvians and ironically, they suffered the same fate as the herd of pigs. There is a sobering end time parallel surrounding Noah and the flood: **"As it was in the days of Noah, so it will be at the coming of the Son of Man."**

Chapter 10

Moses and the Mark of the Beast

The life of Moses could be divided into three distinct segments of 40 years each: The first segment began with his birth and ended with him murdering an Egyptian taskmaster. The next segment began when Moses escaped from Egypt and ended when he returned to Egypt. The final segment of his life began with the Exodus and ended when he died.

Except for his miraculous escape from death shortly after he was born, the Bible gives minimal information about Moses' first 40 years. (See Exodus 1 and 2.) The Bible does not reveal how Pharaoh's daughter adopted Moses or provide additional insight about his time in Pharaoh's house. We do know, however, that when Moses grew to be a man, he refused to be called the son of Pharaoh's daughter. (Hebrews 11:24) The reason Moses murdered the Egyptian taskmaster remains a mystery to me. Did Moses kill the Egyptian out of a sense of injustice or was Moses simply looking for a way to gain respect from his Hebrew brothers? The circumstances surrounding the murder happened this way: One day Moses left the comforts of Pharaoh's palace to see for himself how his Hebrew brothers were fairing under the agony of slavery. He came upon an Egyptian who was beating a Hebrew slave and believing that no one was watching (Exodus 2:12), Moses killed the Egyptian and quickly buried the corpse in the sand. However, another Hebrew witnessed the event and word of the murder spread like a wildfire through the Hebrew camp. Moses feared for his life and fled to the desert to escape Pharaoh's wrath.

For the next segment of 40 years, Moses lived in the desert as a fugitive. While working for minimum wages (tending sheep) in the hostile environment of the desert, Moses discovered two essential elements of life: A *patient* faith in God and contentment. The stark surroundings of the desert with its unforgiving lessons of survival taught Moses more about depending on the Lord than he could have ever learned while living in Pharaoh's palace. Moses also discovered the power and joy of love when he cared for the sheep. Ultimately, the first 80 years of his life prepared Moses for the finest and final segment of his life. His education in Pharaoh's schools and his re-education in the desert combined in a unique way to make him one of the world's finest servant leaders.

The Servant Leader

Being a servant leader is quite difficult because the attitudes of a servant and the attitudes of a leader are constantly at war against each other for mastery. The "leader" uses authority and control to meet objectives, but the "servant" uses love to get the job done. The servant leader exalts the welfare and development of his or her subjects equal to that of the objectives. In other words, the servant aspect of leadership is willing to miss objectives (or profits) to improve and develop the members of the group, whereas the leader aspect of leadership is willing to sacrifice members of the group to meet the objectives! In practice, this balance is very hard to manage and Moses often failed in his attempt to be a servant leader. Remember the time he impatiently struck a rock to obtain water when God had commanded him to speak to it? (Numbers 20:8-12) That impatient act prevented Moses from entering the promised land. I find it ironic that Moses had to flee from Pharaoh's palace because of an impulsive act and he also failed to enter the promised land due to his impulsive nature.

After Moses was gone for 40 years, God forced him to return to Egypt. The Lord's anger burned against Moses because he resisted God's command at the burning bush to return to Egypt! (Exodus 4:14) Shortly after the burning bush episode, Moses made the Lord so angry that the Lord was prepared to kill Moses. In that case, Moses' wife, Zipporah, saved him from God's wrath! (Exodus 4:24) When Moses arrived in Egypt, he

was a much different man than when he left. Moses had left
Egypt with an attitude of a leader, but he returned 40 years
later with an attitude of a servant. A tremendous difference
lies between the egocentric attitude of the young Moses and
the theo-centric attitude of Moses at age 80. It took 40 years of
tending sheep to transform Moses into a meek man. When
Moses finally learned how to follow The Good Shepherd, God
promoted Moses to be a shepherd of God's people.

A Man without a Country

When Moses arrived back in Egypt after his 40-year wilderness sojourn, he did not have the respect of the Hebrew elders.
No doubt, some of the elders remembered that Moses was a
fugitive from justice. This made it necessary for God to use
miraculous signs through Moses in the presence of the elders.
Otherwise, the elders would have rejected Moses and the
message he presented. (Exodus 4:30,31) From our vantage
point today, it is interesting that even after directing a miraculous exodus from Egypt using great displays of God's power,
his people still did not respect Moses. There is a simple reason
for this: The carnal mind does not understand the spiritual
mind. God used 40 years in the wilderness to transform Moses
into a spiritual man. In the carnal world, leaders (politicians)
must maneuver so a majority of important people constantly
admire them or they will be out of a job. When Moses returned
to Egypt, he did not promote himself to be a savior of the
Hebrews, nor did he seek followers or popularity. He did not
arrive with an entourage of servants nor did he command a
mighty army prepared to defeat Pharaoh. Moses arrived in
Egypt as a servant of God. Moses explained to the elders that
the God of Abraham, Isaac and Jacob had sent him back to
Egypt to lead Israel out of Egyptian slavery. To verify Moses'
claim, God worked several miracles through him. (Exodus
4:29-31) After seeing the miracles, the elders believed.

Background

The story of Moses offers several end time parallels that are
important to consider. Interestingly, the parallels found in the

lives of Moses, Pilate, Saul, Esther, Gideon, Daniel and others were recorded in the Bible for *our* benefit! (1 Corinthians 10:11)

For a point of reference, our background study on Moses should begin with Jacob – the great-great grandfather of Moses. Jacob had twelve sons and his favorite son was Rachel's first son, Joseph. (Remember, Jacob worked fourteen years to acquire Rachel from Laban. See Genesis 29.) When Joseph was seventeen, his envious brothers sold him to Midianite merchants for 20 pieces of silver. These merchants took Joseph to Egypt and sold him there as a slave. (Genesis 37:28) In spite of this great injustice, Joseph remained faithful to God, and God wonderfully blessed Joseph through some very tough experiences.

About 23 years after his brothers sold Joseph as a slave, the king of Egypt released him from prison and promoted him to the position of Prime Minster of Egypt. This sudden promotion occurred because God enabled Joseph to interpret a dream that God specifically gave to Pharaoh. Pharaoh's dream predicted seven years of plenty and seven years of famine. God warned Pharaoh of an approaching famine through Joseph, and Pharaoh was so pleased to know the meaning of his dream that he elevated Joseph to his new position. After seven years of bountiful harvests, the sun began to scorch the Earth and the famine was severe and widespread. The famine also reached Canaan and about two years later, Jacob and his eleven sons ran out of food. In desperation, Jacob sent ten of his sons to Egypt to buy food. Through a series of events, Jacob's sons discovered their little brother, Joseph, was the Prime Minister of Egypt. Imagine their great fear and panic! In one of the greatest acts of compassion ever recorded, Joseph forgave his brothers and insisted that his father and all of his brothers move to Egypt. Knowing the famine would last five more years, Joseph moved his father and brothers to the region of Goshen and the children and grandchildren of Jacob (Israel) flourished in Egypt.

One of Jacob's twelve sons, Levi, had a son named Kohath. Now, follow the genealogy – Kohath had a son named Amram, and Amram was the father of Aaron and Moses. This Levi-Kohath-Amram-Moses genealogy is important to this story because Moses knew as a youngster that *his generation – the fourth generation* – was the generation scheduled to be freed from Egyptian slavery! Review the original promise that God gave to Abraham many years earlier: **"Then the Lord said to him, 'Know for certain that your descendants will be strangers in a country not their own, and they will be enslaved and mistreated four hundred years. But I will punish the nation they serve as slaves, and afterward they will come out with great possessions. You, however, will go to your fathers in peace and be buried at a good old age. *In the fourth generation* your descendants will come back here, for the sin of the Amorites has not yet reached its full measure.' "** (Genesis 15:13-16, italics mine)

The Fourth Generation

I hope you have read the Bible account describing how God miraculously used Pharaoh's daughter to rescue baby Moses from the river and adopt him. (Exodus 2) Growing up in the palace of Pharaoh and learning about his miraculous rescue at birth could put all kinds of ideas in a young man's mind. I am sure that as Moses grew into manhood, he probably concluded that *he* was a man of destiny. Moses could easily have concluded that God had chosen *him* to deliver Israel from Pharaoh's control and lead His people into Canaan to inherit the land God promised Abraham. I believe these ideas were probable because at that time, Moses was the only Hebrew in the world who was not a slave. Moses also was aware that he belonged to the fourth generation and knew God had promised Abraham that the fourth generation in Egypt would return to Canaan and inherit the land! Evidently these thoughts led Moses to conclude that *he* was the one who would set his people free. However, one pivotal problem with Moses' conclusion was that the slaves had no respect for Moses. They lived in the ghetto of Goshen and every day they endured terrible suffering as slaves. Conversely, Moses had lived in Pharoah's palace and enjoyed the best things that money could buy. No matter what Moses thought and though Moses refused to be called a son of Pharaoh's daughter (Hebrews 11:24,25), the other Hebrews did not regard Moses *as one of them!* Moses probably knew about this alienation and set out to prove to his kinsmen that he really identified with them and their suffering. Part of Moses' motivation for killing the Egyptian may have been the strained relationship between Moses and his identification with his people. However, the murder was a rash decision and it did not enamor Moses to his people. In reality, his action ultimately proved to everyone that he was not very smart. The very next day, when Moses realized that (a) his own people had no interest in mounting an insurrection against Pharaoh by following his example, and (b) Pharaoh would probably sentence him to death for unlawfully killing an Egyptian, Moses decided it was in his best interest to disappear from Egypt. His grand illusion of delivering the Hebrews from slavery simply evaporated as he fled into the isolation of the desert to save himself from certain death.

End Time Parallel

With God, timing is everything. God did not need Moses to deliver *His* people from slavery. God could have exercised any one of thousands of options to deliver His people. This brings up an interesting point about faith. I believe Moses was like Abraham. Moses wanted to deliver his people from slavery, but God's larger plans for the Exodus included several object lessons between Himself and Pharaoh. Of course, Moses did not know about God's larger picture and Moses' finite view of God's plans led to his failure. **This is always the human problem.** Remember the case of adultery between Abraham and Hagar? Abraham and Sarah schemed to fulfill God's plan by violating their marriage covenant. Moses attempted to fulfill God's magnificent plans by killing an Egyptian. *Like Abraham, Moses sincerely believed in God, but both men failed because they would not wait for God to resolve the situation!*

Moses violated God's law by killing the Egyptian and consequently, he had 40 years of solitary isolation! As a fugitive in the harsh setting of a desert prison, Moses learned submission and total dependance on God. Moses discovered the practical meaning of faith and learned *how* to wait so that God could fulfill His higher purposes for Moses. (Waiting for God is one of the most difficult lessons to learn. James 1:4) When God concluded that Moses' spiritual life had reached a satisfactory level of maturity, He called Moses to do a special work for Him and Moses submitted to God's plan.

There is a profound end time parallel here. During the Great Tribulation, each person will face a question of survival. As the issue of survival becomes all-consuming, *the human solution* will stand opposing *the divine solution*. (Our ways are often contrary to God's ways, because God's ways are not like our ways.) For example, the Bible makes it clear that a severe famine will occur during the Great Tribulation and food supplies will be scarce. So, in the face of death, does hunger justify stealing? The juxtaposition between starvation and stealing forces each of us to take a tough look at the principles we honestly maintain. If we answer "yes" to the question that hunger justifies stealing, then our principles are no different from the principles of thugs who currently roam and loot the world. They steal because they do not have what they want and do not trust God to provide for their needs. Do not stop there – take the question one step further. Does hunger justify killing? If we answer "yes," then we are no different from Moses whose impulsive act killed the Egyptian. The point is that submission to God means submission to *God's control of the situation* – and in some cases this means submission to the point of death. (Remember the three Hebrews in the fiery furnace?) Here is a truth to consider: *Calvary proves that Jesus would not participate in wrong doing (unrighteousness) to sustain His own life (and neither should those who honor Him)!* (See Matthew 4.)

The Great Tribulation is just before us, so carefully consider these words from Revelation 13:10: **"If anyone is to go into**

captivity, into captivity he will go. If anyone is to be
killed with the sword, with the sword he will be killed.
This calls for patient endurance and faithfulness on the
part of the saints.**" Reread that last sentence. This text is
directed at God's people during the Great Tribulation and it
indicates that many of God's people will be imprisoned *without*
justification. Also, many of God's people will be killed *without*
justification. So, get ready children of God. This world is full of
injustice and it will be directed our way soon! God's Word has
declared the course of coming events so that our faith in God
might remain steady. God's people need *patient endurance
and faithfulness!* God knows the future and He already knows
the outcome for each of us. Obviously, we do not know how our
particular future will unfold, but that is not our concern. Our
concern is to remain faith-full to God and the principles of His
kingdom today – even to the point of death!

Moses before Pharaoh

The first time Moses and Aaron approached Pharaoh, they
presented a small *demand*. Notice that God did not demand
something from Pharaoh that would destroy his nation's
economy. God merely demanded a three day leave of absence,
that is all. **". . . Moses and Aaron went to Pharaoh and
said, 'This is what the Lord, the God of Israel, says: "Let
my people go, so that they may hold a festival to me in
the desert.'"** Pharaoh said, 'Who is the Lord, that I
should obey him and let Israel go? I do not know the
Lord and I will not let Israel go.'"** (Exodus 5:1,2)

Pharaoh's response immediately revealed his heart! Although
Pharaoh has been dead for a long time, his words and attitude
live on. The *carnal response* of the human heart when brought
face to face with the sovereign will of God remains unchanged:
"Who is the Lord that I should obey Him?" God did not
offer to negotiate with Pharaoh. Instead, God confronted
Pharaoh with a direct order, **"Let my people go. . . ."** During
the Great Tribulation, God will confront the people of Earth
with a direct order, **". . . Fear God and give him glory,**

because the hour of his judgment has come. *Worship him* who made the heavens, the earth, the sea and the springs of water." (Revelation 14:7, italics mine) Moses and Aaron were to Pharaoh what the 144,000 will be to the world during the Great Tribulation. God will empower and send His servants throughout the world to proclaim the everlasting gospel. The gospel of Christ commands everyone to worship the Creator. This means that we should structure our lives to incorporate the Ten Commandments, which includes His seventh day Sabbath. God's point-blank declaration will produce a similar response to that of Pharaoh in many people. They will say, **"Who is the Lord, that I should obey him. . . ."**

Remember that it took ten plagues to ravage Egypt before Pharaoh's rebellion temporarily softened. Pharaoh's behavior should hold special meaning for students of Bible prophecy, especially for individuals who want to understand the use of "Sodom and Egypt" in Revelation 11:8. Notice the text: **"Their bodies** [e.g., the two witnesses] **will lie in the street of the great city, which is figuratively called Sodom and Egypt, where also their Lord was crucified."** Consider why the Bible refers to Sodom and Egypt in Revelation 11. These two entities, Sodom and Egypt, describe the mind set of the wicked at the time of the seventh trumpet. The seventh trumpet (Revelation 11:15-19) marks the close of the offer of salvation. When the seventh trumpet sounds in Heaven, God will have separated the people of Earth into two groups (sheep and goats). God will seal one group with His seal and the other group will have received the mark of the beast. The group that receives the mark of the beast will have the same defects in their character as the ancient inhabitants of Sodom and Egypt. Sodom represents a class of people who cannot discern right from wrong. The Sodomites *were inebriated with sexual immorality* and they vigorously promoted their degenerate ways. The consciences of the Sodomites and the inhabitants who lived in the cities around Sodom were cauterized as with a hot iron. As a result, God's patient forbearance with them ended and He burned Sodom, Gomorrah and several adjacent cities to the ground with a meteorite shower of burning hail and sulphur. (Genesis 13:13; 19:24-29)

Egypt, on the other hand, represents a class of people who defiantly refuse to submit to God's authority. Like Pharaoh, Egypt represents a group of people who will refuse to render obedience to Almighty God, even after they have heard God's demands! The terms, Sodom and Egypt, represent a point in time when divine forbearance with the wicked has no redemptive effect. When God's subjects have reached that point, God can do no more to save them. Therefore, God will destroy the wicked, just as He did in Pharaoh's day. Think about this: A Sovereign is not sovereign as long as rebellion exists! This is why God will ultimately destroy sin itself! (1 Corinthians 15:24-28)

From Pharaoh's Point of View

It is quite possible to read a page in the Bible and overlook some essential points that are on that page. People who have studied the Bible at length know what I mean. Words are a means to convey thoughts and thoughts are the language of the Spirit! I mention this because I would like to present Pharaoh's response to Aaron and Moses from Pharaoh's point of view. Of course, I have speculated about some details in the story that are not found in Scripture, however, I have conscientiously tried to keep the added information consistent with the historical setting.

One morning, as Pharaoh Amenhotep II was sitting on his throne and overseeing the business of his expansive kingdom, his court secretary informed him that two Hebrews, Aaron and Moses, were present and wanted to speak with him. The king was pleased to hear that these two men wanted to meet with him. Pharaoh had heard rumors about Aaron and Moses and he wanted to confront them! Pharaoh concluded this was a fine opportunity that was knocking at his door.

Ordinarily, slaves were denied access to Pharaoh, since they belonged to the lowest order of Egyptian culture. In Pharaoh's government, lieutenants who managed slaves reported to governors who oversaw the day-to-day operations of the king-dom. If any lieutenant or governor allowed the king to suffer loss, Pharaoh executed or publicly humiliated them. Such was the harsh, but highly effective management style of Amenhotep II. Pharaoh wanted to meet with Aaron and Moses because he had received reports that revealed that these two men had convinced many slaves to rest from their labors on the seventh day of the week. Rebellion is an alarming develop-ment for any king, but Pharaoh was, for the moment, more curious than furious at this recent development among the slaves. He wanted to know what was going on.

So, Pharaoh invited these two elderly men from Goshen into his court. Evidently, Amenhotep II did not know that Moses had killed an Egyptian 40 years earlier. If Amenhotep II had known, the Egyptians would have arrested Moses on the spot as a fugitive from justice. Pharaoh had heard rumors that Moses had supernatural powers and that he could perform miracles. Pharaoh wanted to see Moses himself and verify if this was true. (Exodus 4:29-31) Pharaoh also knew about a prophecy circulating among the slaves that their God had given to their patriarch, Abraham, which stated that Abraham's descendants would serve as slaves in Egypt for 400 years. According to rumor, the slaves believed their 400 years of slavery was about to end. The timing of these reports and the notoriety surrounding Moses aroused Pharaoh's curiosity, so he allowed Aaron and Moses to meet with him.

As Aaron and Moses approached the elevated throne, Pharaoh looked down on two men in their eighties. They were humble and polite; not arrogant or hostile. They respectfully bowed before the king and after expressing appreciation for the audience, they presented the *demand* of their God: ". . . **This is what the Lord, the God of Israel, says: 'Let my people go, so that they may hold a festival to me in the desert.'** " (Exodus 5:1)

Pharaoh was not prepared to hear a demand from two slaves. No doubt he reacted much like any king would have reacted.

Kings typically have huge egos and "demands" are something they give – not something they receive. Pharaoh did not expect the sheer boldness of Aaron and Moses. Pharaoh expected these two slaves to have an attitude closer to begging or groveling. After all, a couple of slaves were talking to the Pharaoh of Egypt. Even more, as a matter of court etiquette, a person does not demand something of a Sovereign. Even Esther humbly *asked* her husband, King Xerxes, to spare her life and the lives of her people from annihilation. (Esther 7:3)

Pharaoh must have smiled or winced at their foolishness. He looked at them for a couple seconds, gathered his thoughts and rose to his feet. He answered their demand with two simple statements. First, he denigrated the God of Israel. **"Who is this Lord, the God of Israel, that I should obey him?"** As a man-god, Pharaoh believed that he had higher authority than the God of Israel. Before you condemn the pompous king, ask yourself if you have ever stood in Pharaoh's sandals. Have you ever defended a belief that you thought was true, only to learn later the belief you supported was dead wrong? Among the religions of the world, which one has the greater God? Is Allah greater than Jehovah? Is Buddha greater than Jesus? Of course, the answer you may give to these questions about the superiority of gods will depend on your beliefs about God. Pharaoh worshiped the sun-god, Ra, and he was convinced his god was superior to the God of Israel. The Egyptians believed that Ra appointed Pharaoh himself to rule over Egypt and Pharaoh believed that Ra had divinely empowered him to be Egypt's king.

Pharaoh truthfully answered: **"I do not know the Lord and I will not let Israel go."** Pharaoh faced the bearers of God's demand and bluntly stated that he would not *obey* the demand. His response was about as direct and to the point as a human being can get – no weasel words from Pharaoh. In his defense, Pharaoh's response reflected his religious beliefs. From his point of view, Ra, was superior to Israel's God because the Hebrew nation was subservient to Egypt. If the God of the Hebrews was greater than Ra, then let Him deliver them from his hand! Now be honest. If you had been in Pharaoh's sandals that day, would you have granted a couple million slaves time off for a three-day religious service after two elderly slaves, speaking for the God of captives, *demanded* it?

The Fear of the Lord

"Then they said [to Pharaoh], **'The God of the Hebrews has met with us. Now let us take a three-day journey into the desert to offer sacrifices to the Lord our God, or he may strike us with plagues or with the sword.'"** (Exodus 5:3) Moses and Aaron were caught between their fear of the Lord and their fear of Pharaoh. They wanted to be sure the king knew they were not requesting a three-day leave of absence simply as a ploy to escape Pharaoh's dominion. Rather, they were presenting a demand that the Lord their God had given to them. Moses and Aaron tried to reason with Pharaoh and told him the Hebrews needed to make atonement for their sins with *their* God or *their* God might destroy them! During 400 years of slavery in Egypt, the Hebrews had largely ignored God because remaining faithful to a God who permits His children to be held captive in a depressing situation that has no apparent end is very difficult. So, God told Israel through His servant, Moses, that His people must atone for their sins, as a precondition for being delivered from slavery. In other words, before a person (or nation) can receive the gift of freedom from slavery (sin), he or she must first make things right with God, then submit to God's demands.

To be honest, I do not think Pharaoh gave their response any thought. He wanted to get down to business. Standing before him were two men who had caused a big administrative problem. Pharaoh said, **". . . Moses and Aaron, why are *you* taking the people away from their labor? Get back to your work!"** (Exodus 5:4, italics mine) The king had heard that Moses and Aaron were the instigators of a Sabbath rest rebellion and he ordered them to stop resting on the seventh day and get back to work. This is quite a story. The story started when Moses notified the Hebrew elders that God required the Hebrews to rest from their labors on His holy day, the seventh day of the week, as another precondition for deliverance from slavery. Every slave was excited to hear that deliverance was at hand and of course, everyone welcomed a day of rest from their labors. So, the elders gave the word and the slaves began to keep God's seventh day Sabbath by resting from their labor. Can you imagine the response of the task masters when they went to work as usual and found no slaves to do the work? So, Pharaoh's lieutenants immediately responded by requiring the slaves to produce the *same* quota of bricks in six days as they had been producing in seven. As far as the lieutenants were concerned, this requirement ensured the same level of production each week as before. The slaves did not complain, even though the observance of Sabbath meant extra hours of work each day – doing the work of seven days in six days.

> **NOTE:** Scholars have debated whether the work stoppage caused by Moses and Aaron was the observance of God's seventh day Sabbath. Even though Exodus 5 does not specifically say the slaves rested on the seventh day of the week, the harmony of four supporting points adequately resolves this question.
>
> 1. From Creation to the time God gave the Ten Commandments at Mt. Sinai (a period of about 2,500 years), the only day set aside for rest is God's Sabbath, the seventh day of the week. (Genesis 2:2,3; Exodus 20:8-11)
>
> 2. Before God spoke the Ten Commandments on Mt. Sinai, He tested Israel to see if they would obey Him by observing His seventh day. (Exodus 16:4.) This test proves two things. First, God's seventh day was holy *before* God gave the Ten Commandments. (Genesis 2:1-3) Second, God required Israel to observe His Sabbath *before* He gave the Ten Commandments.
>
> 3. God demands that His subjects observe His Sabbath day as written in the fourth commandment because worshiping God cannot be determined by reason, customs, traditions or culture. True worship is joyful submission to God's *demands*. The Ten Commandments are not ten suggestions; the Ten Commandments are ten laws. Some scholars argue that Sabbath observance was an idea codified in the Ten Com-

mandments to benefit the children of Israel. If this argument were true, why did God declare the seventh day of the week to be "holy" (or set apart) to Adam and Eve? (Genesis 2:1-3)

4. The word Pharaoh used suggests that Moses and Aaron led Israel to *Sabbath* from their labors. In Exodus 5:5, Pharaoh said to Aaron and Moses "**. . . You make them rest from their labor**" (KJV) and "**. . . You are stopping them from working. . . .**" (NIV) This verse indicates two things: First, Pharaoh appropriately charges Aaron and Moses for causing the Israelites to cease their labor. Think about this. Did Aaron and Moses cause Israel to rest from making bricks to agitate Pharaoh or did the slaves submit to the Sabbath rest because it was God's holy day? Second, the Hebrew word used by Pharaoh is *shabath* (Strong's #7673). He said, ". . . You make them *shabath*. . . ." This is the same word God used in Genesis 2:2 when He *rested* from His creative work on the seventh day. Furthermore, the Hebrew word for "Sabbath" in the fourth commandment is a derivative of *shabath* — the word Pharaoh used.

The combination of these four points indicates that the Hebrews were not honoring God's Sabbath day as they knew God had commanded, and He told Moses that they must worship Him by keeping His Sabbath day holy if they wanted to be delivered. (See Ezekiel 20:7,8.) So, the slaves obediently began to rest on the seventh day. Allegiance to God's demand put Israel in direct opposition to Pharaoh's demand! This is exactly what God wanted and the end time parallel to this story will be no different. When it comes to worshiping God – faith, obedience and deliverance are inseparable. It is impossible for a person knowingly to defy God's sovereignty and simultaneously, enjoy God's favor. Moses informed the Hebrew elders that Israel must prove its faith in God to be delivered from slavery. Their first step in faith was to rest on God's Sabbath. Israel had to submit to God's higher authority to be delivered from slavery. God tested Israel's faith because His higher law conflicted with Pharaoh's lesser law. The distinct end time parallel should be obvious.

Pharaoh Becomes Mean

"That same day Pharaoh gave this order to the slave drivers and foremen in charge of the people: 'You are no

longer to supply the people with straw for making
bricks; let them go and gather their own straw. But
require them to make the same number of bricks as
before; don't reduce the quota. They are lazy; that is
why they are crying out, "Let us go and sacrifice to our
God." ' " (Exodus 5:6-8) After Aaron and Moses departed,
Pharaoh reacted hatefully to their visit. God knew this was
coming. Pharaoh became mean because he had no intention of
losing control of the slaves. Notice how the carnal heart oper-
ates: Selfishness is all about getting and gaining, not losing.
Ego is all about being in control, not losing control. The threat
of loss produces anxiety and anger in the carnal heart. Aaron
and Moses pressed Pharaoh's big red panic button, and his
immediate response was to inflict a great deal of pain on his
slaves. Pharaoh's response did not surprise God. God knew this
was coming.

Please understand three things about living by faith. First,
faith in God is much more than believing something about God
is true. Agreeing with truth is different from living by faith.
(Even the demons know certain truths about God – and
tremble. James 2:19) Faith in God means obedient submission
to God's will *at any cost.*

Second, a life of faith is a life of testing. God's law is higher
than man's law and He seriously tests faith when we are
caught between doing right (as man decrees) or right (as God
decrees) – especially when the penalty for violating either law
is severe. Daniel demonstrated this point when he was lowered into the lion's den. He violated the king's law and he was
to die in the lion's den. (Daniel 6) The story of Meshach,
Shadrach and Abednego also demonstrates this point. These
men were about to die (or so they thought) for honoring God's
law and violating the king's law. (Daniel 3) Many people
misunderstand what it means to have faith in God. God's law
demands a level of righteousness that no human can achieve.
The good news of the gospel is that God has eliminated our
condemnation if we are willing to live by faith in Christ Jesus.
This does not mean that God has eliminated His law. Instead,

it means that God will cover our imperfections with Christ's righteousness if we are willing to submit to His laws that are above all other laws. (Romans 7 and 8)

The third component of living by faith concerns ignorance. Ignorance is no excuse for disobedience in man's laws. You may drive 65 mph on a highway, honestly thinking that it is the speed limit. Not until an officer of the law stops and tells you that the speed limit is 55 mph and writes a speeding ticket, do you realize your error. When it comes to God's law, ignorance does not lessen the consequences of sin, but ignorance does cancel the guilt. In this regard, God is much more generous than man because He knows our heart. But, remember that God will not, under any circumstances, pardon a person who lives in a defiant state of disobedience. (Hebrews 10:26) God confronted Pharaoh with the sovereignty of a higher King and his stubborn defiance eventually brought about condemnation and destruction.

These three points are inserted so you can see how God dealt with Pharaoh, who *at first, was ignorant* of God's sovereignty. He honestly believed that the God of the Hebrews was a lesser God than his sun-god, Ra. However, when the evidence of God's superiority became overwhelming, Pharaoh's ignorance did not give way to submission. Instead, it turned into open defiance. Pharaoh's experience translates into a powerful end time parallel. Currently, billions of people are ignorant of God's demands on the human race. During the Great Tribulation, God will present His demands in the clearest of terms to the human race. Some people will submit to God's demands, but a large majority of people will make the transition from ignorance to defiance.

Countermeasures

To counteract what he thought to be the religious nonsense spread by Aaron and Moses, Pharaoh imposed his authority on the slaves to painfully remind them of his sovereignty. Pharaoh demanded more work from the slaves than they could produce and his demands translated into immediate suffering.

Pharaoh's lieutenants controlled the slaves through a very
clever scheme. Hebrew elders were appointed over family
work units. Whenever a work unit failed to meet its quota, the
elders were publicly beaten while their family work unit
watched. This form of terrorism controlled the Hebrews very
well. It was too much for sons and grandsons, daughters and
granddaughters, to see their fathers beaten when production
was inadequate, so they worked "like slaves" to meet their
quotas.

Pharaoh imposed his demand on the Hebrews the very day
that Moses and Aaron presented God's demand to the king.
What a knee jerk reaction! Consider the developing dilemma:
God demanded Sabbath rest as a precondition for deliverance,
and Pharaoh demanded greater work and higher quotas from
the slaves. In addition to producing the same quota of bricks
as before, they now had to gather the straw — an impossible
demand! This meant the elders of each family would be beaten
regularly since the quotas could not be met. Suddenly, God's
Sabbath became a nightmare. How could the slaves spend
Sabbath with any peace of mind knowing that Sabbath rest
would produce ruthless beatings? Even if the slaves did not
observe the seventh day Sabbath rest, they now had to gather
straw to make their bricks. This chore was not required of
them before Moses came to town. So, the work load reached a
new high and their despair reached a new low. Their hopes of
deliverance were crushed by intense suffering.

"Leave Us Alone Moses!"

A group of elders went to Pharaoh's court and with one voice
they begged him to be reasonable and lighten the work load
because it was humanly impossible for them to fulfill the
demand. The Bible says, **"The Israelite foremen realized
they were in trouble when they were told, 'You are not
to reduce the number of bricks required of you for each
day.' When they left Pharaoh, they found Moses and
Aaron waiting to meet them, and they said, 'May the
Lord look upon you and judge you! You have made us a**

stench to Pharaoh and his officials and have put a sword in their hand to kill us.' " (Exodus 5:19-21) Aaron and Moses must have felt terrible. A simple demand presented to Pharaoh had turned life for the Hebrews upside down. Of course, God foreknew these events would occur, but He wanted to demonstrate several key parallels about Pharaoh's carnal heart *for future generations.* People can joyfully declare allegiance to God when there is no contest between the laws of men and the laws of God. Keeping God's Sabbath rest is a joy when there is no threat of persecution. However, sooner or later, God's sovereignty collides with governments of this world. The Bible says there was war in Heaven over the issue of God's sovereignty. (See Isaiah 14 and Revelation 12.) The struggle for supremacy is the essence of the battle – whether the battlefield is the human heart, the court of Pharaoh, or in Heaven. The battle to control human loyalty has never been more intense than it is right now, and most people are unaware that it is even going on! The devil knows that his days are short and he is working overtime to keep the minds of people dull with the cares of life. The devil has lured young people into sexual immorality and he has pacified "pew warmers" with entertainers who have no idea of God's coming wrath. The day when God will suddenly step into the affairs of the human race and reveal His sovereignty is almost here. On a single day, life on Earth will change! (Revelation 8:2-5)

God is about to send a series of devastating judgments on the Earth (the seven trumpets of Revelation) and during these judgments, through His 144,000 servants, He will announce His will to Earth's inhabitants. Revelation predicts that most men and women will respond like Pharaoh: **"I do not know the Lord and I will not obey. . . ."** When Moses saw the elders being beaten because they could not meet their quota of bricks, **"Moses returned to the Lord and said, 'O Lord, why have *you* brought trouble upon this people? Is this why you sent me? Ever since I went to Pharaoh to speak in your name, he has brought trouble upon this people, and you have not rescued your people at all.' "** (Exodus 5:22,23, italics mine) Moses had presented God's demands before Pharaoh just as God required. Imagine how Moses must have felt when he saw the painful beatings. No wonder Moses cried unto the Lord, "*You* have not helped *your* people! *You* are killing them with the rod of Pharaoh!" If only Moses had understood that this was exactly the situation the Lord wanted. **"Then the Lord said to Moses, 'Now you will see what I will do to Pharaoh: Because of my mighty hand he will let them go; because of my mighty hand he will drive them out of his country.' "** (Exodus 6:1) God's purposes and actions are always manifold. In a spiritual sense, this means that God "kills several birds with one stone." His ways are always higher and grander than our earthly solutions. **"As the heavens are higher than the Earth, so are my ways higher than your ways and my thoughts than your thoughts."** (Isaiah 55:9) God is the Master Designer and Moses' story has many lessons and parallels for you and me.

Summary Parallels

1. The sovereignty of God is a truth and man's awareness of this fact is ever evaporating. Lessons learned yesterday are forgotten tomorrow. Unless we are careful, we can minimize God's power and like young Moses and Abraham, take matters into our own hands and dishonor Him. The problem with fallen humanity is that we are always trying to assume the prerogatives of God. To compensate for this sinister process, from time to time, God creates real-life dramas with real-life players to remind every person of His sovereignty. Remember how King Nebuchadnezzar vainly thought he was Sovereign over Earth? After living like an animal for seven years, he finally conceded that God was Sovereign. Pharaoh, on the other hand, refused to concede that God was Sovereign, even after God horribly decimated Egypt with ten plagues! Pharaoh went to his death (in the middle of the Red Sea) because of his defiant stubbornness. Pharaoh's experience proves that rebellion can be so complete within a person's heart that he or she will never submit to God. The truth remains, however, that no sooner is the knowledge of God's authority established on Earth than it begins to evaporate again.

When God created the seventh day, He had His reasons for doing so. God imposed His Sabbath rest test on the Hebrews to show His Sovereign power to the Hebrews and the Egyptians. It is a mystery that so many people do not want to rest on God's Sabbath. People offer a dozen reasons why we should not observe God's Sabbath, but what are excuses to God? When God demanded that His Sabbath be observed as a precondition for deliverance, the Hebrews initially complied. When Pharaoh learned that the Israelites threatened his sovereignty, he implemented pain and torture. The slaves were trapped between two great powers and the penalty for defying either was great!

During the Great Tribulation, God will present His Sabbath rest to the people of Earth with the force of law. God's servants, the 144,000, will explain how God's seventh day Sabbath is not a suggestion, nor an option – it is the fourth commandment of God's law. Like Pharaoh, the world does not currently submit to God's law or honor God's day of rest. During the Great Tribulation, a great conflict will erupt over the issue of worship. Bible prophecies reveal how this conflict will occur: God will initiate the Great Tribulation with a series of destructive judgments. Because these coming judgments will be overwhelming and catastrophic (killing more than 1.5 billion people in a short time), the survivors on Earth will suddenly wake up to the reality that there is a living God and He is angry with man's behavior. To appease God so that His judgments will cease, the religious and political leaders of the world will unite and impose sinless laws upon mankind. Eventually, these laws will include laws *mandating* that God be worshiped, but these laws will directly oppose God's law. This contest that God has ordained will cause the people of Earth (like the Hebrews of old) to be caught between two powerful forces. If people obey the laws of men, they will receive the seven bowls of God's wrath. (Revelation 16) If people obey God's law and honor His seventh day Sabbath, the governments of the world will persecute, imprison or execute them for rebellion. This is the coming contest, and the story of Moses offers an end time parallel for God's people so that our faith in God is strengthened for this eventuality.

2. Remember that God demanded the Hebrews to observe His Sabbath as a precondition for deliverance. God sent this demand through Moses because He wanted to (a) demonstrate man's rebellion by confronting Pharaoh, the most powerful man on Earth at the time, (b) teach the Hebrews their first lesson in faith, e.g., the importance of trusting in God's leading at any cost or suffering, and (c) use Israel and their deliverance as an object lesson for generations to come. Unfortunately, Pharaoh's persecution destroyed the faith of most Hebrews. They lost confidence in Moses and in God. So, God sent them a message of hope: **"Therefore [Moses], say to the Israelites: 'I am the Lord, and I will bring you out from under the yoke of the Egyptians. I will free you from being slaves to them, and I will redeem you with an outstretched arm and with mighty acts of judgment. I will take you as my own people, and I will be your God. *Then you will know that I am the Lord your God*, who brought you out from under the yoke of the Egyptians. And I will bring you to the land I swore with uplifted hand to give to Abraham, to Isaac and to Jacob. I will give it to you as a possession. I am the Lord.' Moses reported this to the Israelites, but they did not listen to him because of their discouragement and cruel bondage."** (Exodus 6:6-9, italics mine) Did you notice the last sentence? The Hebrews murmured against Almighty God, gave Moses a good cussing and refused to go along with God's plans. If the Hebrews could have known all that we know now, they would have rejoiced at God's words! However, no murmuring, faithlessness, discouragement, and bitterness can shut out God's promises and purposes.

There is an end time parallel here. God placed the Hebrews in a tough situation to test their faith and He showed them they had no faith. Unfortunately, they did not catch the vision and they gave up! Most of the Hebrews went back to work on Sabbath because they lacked faith in God. Do not forget, these same people died in the wilderness because they never over-came their lack of faith. The end time parallel here is so powerful. Believers in Christ are now the Hebrews. We are the children of God! During the Great Tribulation, God will once again set His Sabbath rest up in direct opposition to man's laws. Everyone who wants to be delivered from the bondage of sin must submit to God as a precondition to being set free! This will cause our faith to be severely tested. Salvation comes through faith and God will test our faith to see where each of us will stand! When people deliberately and intentionally choose to suffer because of their faith in God, He makes their faith pure, like gold. This refining process produces the type of people who will inherit the Earth made new! God says, **"This third** [the remnant] **I will bring into the fire; I will refine them like silver and test them like gold. They will call on my name and I will answer them; I will say, 'They are my people,' and they will say, 'The Lord is our God.' "** (Zechariah 13:9, insertion mine)

3. This study of Moses and the Exodus gives us one final unexpected parallel. For thousands of years, slaves have been marked with tattoos or hot-iron brands. (For a picture of a hot iron used for branding slaves during the era of African slave trading, see *National Geographic*, September 1992, page 72) A person cannot remove or lose a brand or tattoo. It is not trans-ferable. Even as late as World War II, Hitler tattooed millions of prisoners in his concentration camps. The reason for mark-ing slaves is simple. The owner/slave relationship is perma-nent. Children born of slaves are also slaves. Normally, a slave is never freed because ownership never ends. This is the ugly power of slavery (sin). I believe that Pharaoh's adult slaves were marked with tattoos or brands. This mark pre-vented any possibility of escape from Egypt, for no one would dare purchase property belonging to the Egyptian Pharaoh.

Did God forbid the Hebrews from wearing tattoos because they were no longer slaves? He said, **"Do not cut your bodies for the dead or put tattoo marks on yourselves. I am the Lord."** (Leviticus 19:28) Perhaps the reason behind this command is that God's people are never slaves, because they are always free to exercise the power of choice. God did not want His people to deface their bodies with markings associated with slavery. The Lord said, "... **I am the Lord, and I will bring you out from under the yoke of the Egyptians. I will free you from being slaves to them, and I will redeem you with an outstretched arm and with mighty acts of judgment. I will take you as my own people, and I will be your God. Then you will know that I am the Lord your God, who brought you out from under the yoke of the Egyptians.**" (Exodus 6:6,7)

When Pharaoh's firstborn was killed during Passover night, he finally came to the point of temporary submission. He allowed Moses and the children of Israel to leave Egypt at sunrise. To commemorate this marvelous deliverance, God instituted an annual memorial of this event. He told the Israelites, **"This observance** [e.g., the observance of Passover] **will be for you like a sign on your hand and a reminder on your forehead that the law of the Lord is to be on your lips. For the Lord brought you out of Egypt with his mighty hand."** (Exodus 13:9, insertion mine) Another interesting parallel is that observing Passover (the day their freedom began) *was like a sign* on the hand or forehead. This statement may reflect the fact that Pharaoh's slaves wore a sign (a tattoo or branding) on their hand or their foreheads indicating their status. I believe a Hebrew *fore*man probably wore the mark on his *fore*head, while the rank and file slave wore their status on their hands. The parallel is that the mark of the beast will be a tattoo or a branding that will be worn on the right hand or on the forehead! **"He** [the Antichrist, the lamb-like beast] **also forced everyone, small and great, rich and poor, free and slave, to receive a mark on his right hand or on his forehead, so that no one could buy or sell unless he had the mark, which is the name of the** [Antichrist, the lamb-like] **beast or the number of his name."** (Revelation 13:16,17, insertions mine)

When the devil radiantly appears on Earth (fifth trumpet), he will masquerade as God. He will establish a new world order and install himself as king of kings and lord of lords. Only those people who unite with his government can conduct commerce, survival buying and selling. (Revelation 13:17) Anyone who refuses to unite with the devil's one-world government will be killed. The permit to conduct business will be a physical mark on the hand or forehead. The mark will be a tattoo or hot-iron brand. This mark will not be transferrable, so it cannot be stolen or lost. This "proof of membership" in the new world order requires no electricity or computers. This form of identification will work in any village on this planet. Satan's foremen will wear the *name* that the Antichrist will assume on their foreheads, and rank and file members will wear the evil number, 666, on their right hand. To survive, people will submit to the devil's demands rather than submit to the authority of God!

When Jesus comes in clouds of glory, two groups of people will be on Earth: People who chose to receive the mark of the beast and people who are free of Satan's bondage. When Israel finally entered the promised land after 40 years of wandering in the wilderness, the new generation did not bear the marks of slavery on their bodies. They were truly free! On the other hand, the same adults whom God miraculously delivered from Egypt died in the wilderness. Even though they were freed of Pharaoh's slavery by God's mighty power, they never did escape the bondage of their carnal rebellion against God. This is a profound lesson from Moses' story: Our escape from the bondage of sin is only possible through a patient faith that produces total submission to God's demands.

Warning!
Revelation is about to be fulfilled

Warning! Revelation is about to be fulfilled outlines Revelation's story in an easy to read format. Revelation predicts and describes many incredible events that will soon occur. These events will not happen in random order nor will they be freak manifestations of violent weather.

The coming events predicted in Revelation are carefully designed and executed by the Creator of Heaven and Earth.

To learn more about what the prophecies of Daniel and Revelation have to say about coming events, contact the Wake Up America Seminars office at (800) 475-0876 or access the Wake Up America Seminars web site at *http://www.wake-up.org.*

Wake Up America Seminars, Inc.
P.O. Box 273
Bellbrook, OH   45305
http://www.wake-up.org

Jesus
The Alpha and The Omega

Jesus, The Alpha and The Omega provides a basic framework to understand Bible prophecy. This f r a m e w o r k , based on five essential Bible doctrines, helps the serious student of Bible prophecy appreciate the prophecies of Daniel and Revelation. This compelling book examines Jesus' character, ministry, and example. Cross-references to Bible texts provide a basis for in-depth Bible study. This 280 page book can be yours by contacting Wake Up America Seminars at (800) 475-0876.

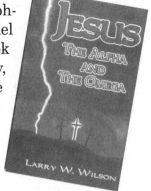

Other Books by Larry Wilson. . .

Daniel Unlocked for the Final Generation
A Study on the Seven Seals and the 144,000
A Study on the Seven Trumpets, Two Witnesses,
    and Four Beasts
17 End-Time Bible Prophecies (coming soon)

Wake Up America Seminars, Inc.
P.O. Box 273
Bellbrook, OH   45305
http://www.wake-up.org

Taped Seminar Series

Many seminar series presented by Larry Wilson have been recorded on CDs and DVDs. Call for a free catalog from the Wake Up America Seminars office at (800) 475-0876. Many recorded subjects are available including presentations on Daniel, Revelation, righteousness by faith, the sanctuary, the plan of salvation, the book of Hebrews, God's justice and mercy, and a study on the great clocks of God.

Wake Up America Seminars, Inc.
P.O. Box 273
Bellbrook, OH   45305
http://www.wake-up.org

About the Author

Larry Wilson, Director of Wake Up America Seminars, became a born again Christian after returning from a tour of duty in Vietnam. The understanding of the gospel, the plan of salvation, and the atonement of Jesus Christ has thrilled his soul for the past 30 years. Since his conversion, he has spent over 30 years intensely studying the Bible.

In 1988, he published the first edition of the book *Warning! Revelation is about to be fulfilled* and since then, has written several books (over 800,000 books in circulation throughout the world in more than 60 countries). He also writes a feature Bible study in the *Day Star* (a monthly publication produced by Wake Up America Seminars). He gives seminar presentations, produces video programs which have been broadcast from various locations throughout the United States, and is a guest on radio talk shows.

About the Organization

Wake Up America Seminars (WUAS) is both a non-profit and a non-denominational organization. With God's blessings and the generosity of many people, WUAS has distributed millions of pamphlets, books and tapes around the world since it began in 1988. WUAS is not a church, nor is it affiliated or sponsored by any religious organization. WUAS does not offer membership of any kind. Its mission is not to convert the world to a point of view. Although WUAS has well defined views on certain biblical matters, its mission is primarily "seed sowing." It promotes the primacy of salvation through faith in Jesus Christ, His imminent return, and is doing its best to encourage people with the good news of the gospel. People of all faiths are invited to study the materials produced by WUAS.

We would like to receive your comments or questions about this book. Please send them to us at the address below. Thank you.

Wake Up America Seminars, Inc.
P.O. Box 273
Bellbrook, OH   45305
http://www.wake-up.org
email: *wuas@wake-up.org*